# Dred Scott:

## person or property?

SUPREME COURT MILESTONES

# Dred Scott:

## person or property?

### Corinne J. Naden
### and Rose Blue

**Benchmark Books**

MARSHALL CAVENDISH
NEW YORK

*With special thanks to Professor David M. O'Brien of the Woodrow Wilson Department of Politics at the University of Virginia for reviewing the text of this book*

Benchmark Books · Marshall Cavendish · 99 White Plains Road · Tarrytown, NY 10591
www.marshallcavendish.com · Copyright © 2005 by Corinne J. Naden and Rose Blue
All rights reserved. No part of this book may be reproduced or utilized in any form or by
any means electronic or mechanical including photocopying, recording, or by any
information storage and retrieval system, without permission from the copyright holders.
Library of Congress Cataloging-in-Publication Data · Naden, Corinne. · Dred Scott :
person or property? / by Corinne J. Naden and Rose Blue. · p. cm. — (Supreme Court
milestones) · Includes bibliographical references and index. · Contents: A slave asks
for freedom — The way it was — A case for judicial restraint — The "worst" decision — The
long path to justice. · ISBN 0-7614-1841-5 · 1. Scott, Dred, 1809–1858—Trials, litigation, etc.—Juvenile literature. 2. Sanford, John F. A., 1806- or 7-1857—Trials, litigation,
etc.—Juvenile literature. 3. Slavery—United States—Legal status of slaves in free states—
Juvenile literature. 4. Slavery—Law and legislation—United States—History—Juvenile literature. [1. Scott, Dred, 1809–1858—Trials, litigation, etc. 2. Slavery—Law and legislation.] I. Naden, Corinne J. II. Title. III. Series. · KF228.S27B58 2004 · 342.7308'7—
dc22 · 2003025568

All Internet sites were available and accurate when sent to press.

Photo Research by Candlepants Incorporated

Cover Photo: Library of Congress (#LC-USZ62-79305)

The photographs in this book are used by permission and through the courtesy of:
Missouri Historical Society, St. Louis: Painting by Louis Schultze, 1, 3, 6, 90; 2,10,
41; Library of Congress: (#LC-USZ62-79305) 19, (#LC-USZ62-126971) 47, (#LC-
USZ6214827) 79, (#LC-USZ-62-78313) 108; Dred Scott, filed April 6, 1846 Circuit
Court Case Files Office of the Circuit Clerk City of St. Louis, Missouri [(2004),
http://stlcourtrecords.wustl.edu]: 21; Corbis: Bettmann, 24, 34, 61; 33, 97, 100;
Getty Images: 44; Collection of the Supreme Court of the United States: 55, 64; Print
Collection, Miriam and Ira D. Wallach Division of Art, Prints and Photographs, The
New York Public Library, Astor, Lenox and Tilden Foundations: 73; Art Resource,
NY: National Portrait Gallery, Smithsonian Institution: 74; The New York Public
Libary, 102; National Archives/Ourdocuments.org: 86.

Series design by Sonia Chaghatzbanian
Printed in China
1 3 5 6 4 2

# contents

A slave, originally known as Sam, then Dred Scott, was at the center of the Supreme Court's "worst" decision.

# one
# A SLAVE ASKS FOR FREEDOM

AT FIRST GLANCE, IT SEEMED a simple matter. In 1834 a slave called Dred Scott was taken from a slave state by his master to live for a time in a free state. After the master died, Scott sued for his freedom on the grounds that he had lived in a free state and that living there made him a free man. The lower court agreed, basing its decision on earlier cases in which slaves who had lived in a free state won their freedom under the legal principle of "once free, always free." But the Missouri State Court overturned the ruling. Dred Scott's lawyers appealed the decision, and by 1857 the case had traveled its slow way through the legal system to the U.S. Supreme Court. The chief justice of the Court, in agreeing with Missouri's finding, wrote: "Negroes had no rights which any white man was bound to respect, and the Negro might justly and lawfully be reduced to slavery for his benefit."

Some critics have called this decision the worst ever handed down by the Supreme Court of the United States. It played a role in bringing on the Civil War because it unleashed deep emotions about race relations. Politically, it was a clear victory for the slaveholding South. It stands as a model of failed judicial statesmanship. It "provided a basis for far-reaching interpretations of substantive due

7 88.666

process." Due process means the law of the land. (Substantive due process, a basic guarantee of the U.S. Constitution, stems from the English idea of a fundamental but unwritten constitution that guarantees individual liberties. This decision negated that guarantee.) For all these reasons, the Dred Scott case is one of the most important decisions in U.S. constitutional history.

At the conclusion of *Scott* v. *Sandford* in 1857, the decision not only denied Dred Scott his freedom, but also the rights of citizenry in his own country. In addition, it struck down the Missouri Compromise of 1820, which tried to ease the conflict over slavery by allowing Missouri to enter the Union as a slave state and Maine as a free state. Voiding the compromise allowed slavery to expand into formerly free territories. It contributed to civil war. In the midst of this turmoil was one black man living in America and making what seemed a simple request.

## A slave named sam

According to many historians, the Dred Scott of *Scott* v. *Sandford* was actually a slave named Sam. The estate of a slave owner, one Peter Blow, lists a Sam who was sold to pay debts about the year 1833. It is believed Sam is the same slave who came to be known as Dred Scott and ended up having his fate decided by the U.S. Supreme Court. Scott was born sometime around 1800 in Southhampton County, Virginia. His exact birth date is unknown because his parents were illiterate slaves and because his owners, Peter and Elizabeth Blow, did not record his birth, as was normal at that time. Scott also grew up illiterate, never learning to do more than mark an X for his signature, a situation not unusual for slaves in the South. Practically nothing is known about Scott's character or early life. A St. Louis newspaper at the time wrote that Scott was "illiterate but not ignorant" with "strong common sense."

Although it is not known whether Blow was Scott's original owner, Scott went along when the Blow family moved to St. Louis in 1830. In Missouri the Blows fell on hard times: Peter's boardinghouse business did not do well and Elizabeth became ill and died in 1831. Following Peter's death the next year, Scott was sold to help pay claims against the estate.

The man who bought Dred Scott, sometime before December 1833, was Dr. John Emerson of St. Louis. Emerson received a commission as assistant surgeon in the U.S. Army in December. Shortly after, Emerson reported for duty at Fort Armstrong in Illinois and took Scott with him. According to the Northwest Ordinance of 1787, slavery was illegal in the state of Illinois, but Emerson apparently ignored that fact. The ordinance prohibited slavery in all United States territories north and west of the Ohio River. In addition to Illinois, this included the present states of Ohio, Indiana, Michigan, Wisconsin, and part of Minnesota.

There are no records to show whether slave and master liked each other or got along well. Emerson, who was about Scott's age, had studied medicine at the University of Pennsylvania. He had always wanted to join the military, but it took considerable influence to get in. With an army of only about six thousand men, there was not a great call for medical officers. However, Emerson proved to be as good a lobbyist as he was a doctor. He got many influential people, including Missouri Senator Thomas Hart Benton, to request his commission. All during his military service, Emerson apparently suffered from a variety of ailments. Records show he requested many leaves of absence and trans-fers, and he died at the early age of forty. His life was

HARRIET ROBINSON WAS LESS THAN HALF THE AGE OF THE MAN WHO LATER BECAME KNOWN AS DRED SCOTT. AS SCOTT'S WIFE, SHE ALSO BECAME THE PROPERTY OF THE MAN WHO OWNED HIM.

undistinguished except for the fame his slave later brought him.

Life was probably not hard for Scott as Emerson's personal servant on an army base. But in 1836 Emerson was transferred when the army closed Fort Armstrong. The new post was Fort Snelling, near present-day St. Paul, Minnesota, on the west bank of the Mississippi. Just weeks before Emerson and Scott arrived, the Wisconsin Enabling Act was passed. It created the Wisconsin Territory, which included the modern states of Wisconsin, Minnesota, and Iowa. The Missouri Compromise of 1820 had already forbidden slavery in new territory, but this new act enforced the ban. So, in effect, Dred Scott had spent two years as a slave in a free state and was now taken to a region where slavery was not allowed.

No one seemed to care. No official, military or civilian, tried to enforce the ban against slavery. As for Scott, he might not have known that slavery was illegal in the territory.

## Marriage and Change

Fort Snelling was a small place. Scott soon met Harriet Robinson, a young slave girl who was probably not even half his age. She was possibly seventeen, and he was nearing forty. Harriet was owned by Major Lawrence Taliaferro (pronounced "Tolliver"), the resident agent overseeing the rights and affairs of Native Americans. Details about Harriet's early years are very sketchy, but she was probably born in Virginia, Taliaferro's home state, and went with him when he was transferred to Bedford, Pennsylvania, and then Fort Snelling. Also the local justice of the peace, Taliaferro married Robinson and Scott, a union that would last for more than twenty years, until Scott's death. When Scott married, according to slavery practices, Harriet also became one of Emerson's slaves. Emerson would eventually acquire the Scotts' two daughters, who would later become part of the suit for freedom.

Emerson detested Fort Snelling; he said it gave him rheumatism. He requested a transfer to St. Louis but instead was called to duty at Fort Jesup, in western Louisiana, late in 1837. He left Scott and his wife behind, hiring them out to fellow officers. Jesup's damp climate apparently made Emerson's rheumatism worse, so he requested a transfer back.

While he was waiting to transfer, Emerson found time for a social life. He met Eliza Irene (known as Irene) Sanford of St. Louis, who was visiting her sister and brother-in-law at Fort Jesup. Sanford and Emerson were married on February 6, 1838. Shortly afterward, he sent for the Scotts, who arrived by steamboat in the spring.

Still wanting to get out of Louisiana, Emerson began another series of letters to the surgeon general requesting transfer. His delicate health was not his only reason. He was having some legal troubles over land he owned near Davenport, Iowa, and wanted to be up north. Oddly, he wrote in a letter on July 10, 1838, "Even one of my negroes in Saint Louis has sued me for his freedom." The reason for that statement has never been explained, since no record of such a suit was ever found and Scott was presumably in Louisiana with Emerson, not in St. Louis, at the time.

The surgeon general finally granted Emerson's transfer request, and in October he and the Scotts were back at Fort Snelling. Once again, Scott was taken as a slave into territory where slavery was illegal. On the steamboat journey back north, Scott's wife gave birth to their first child, who was named Eliza after Emerson's wife. "Thus," according to one historian, "Eliza Scott was born on a boat in the Mississippi River, surrounded on one side by the free state of Illinois and on the other side by the free territory of Wisconsin."

This tour at Fort Snelling did not last very long either. Emerson got into a fight with the base quartermaster, who refused to give him a stove that he had ordered for Scott. The quartermaster struck Emerson and broke his glasses. Emerson returned shortly—waving two pistols. The quartermaster ran away and Emerson was arrested by the post commander. Whether or not that confrontation was the reason, Emerson was transferred to Florida in the spring of 1840.

On his way south, Emerson left his wife and the Scotts in St. Louis to wait for him. He probably did not want them on the new assignment because the Second Seminole War (1835–1842) was still going on. This war was one of three conflicts between the United States and the Seminole Indians that ultimately resulted in the defeat of the Seminoles.

Although Emerson spent almost two and a half years in Florida, within a few months of his arrival, still complaining about his health, he started a new campaign of letters to the surgeon general asking for transfer to St. Louis or elsewhere. Instead, the military gave Emerson an honorable discharge in August 1842, and he was sent home. In the meantime, back in St. Louis, Dred Scott had been seeing the Blow family on the many occasions when some members visited Irene Emerson, especially the third son, Taylor, who would later help in the slave's fight for freedom.

Although Emerson returned to St. Louis, once again he found it difficult to settle down there. He decided to move to a new place to set up a medical practice. So he and his wife, who was expecting a child, moved to Davenport. While their house was being constructed, the Emersons lived in a hotel. Henrietta Emerson was born in late 1843. Her father died on December 29, a month after her birth. The cause of death was noted as consumption, although that diagnosis is not certain. During that time, Dred and Harriet Scott had been left in St. Louis, where they worked for various people.

## Emerson's Last Will

John Emerson left his entire estate to his wife and after her death to his daughter. He also named his wife's brother, John F. A. Sanford of St. Louis, and a friend in Iowa as executors. Sanford was a successful businessman, but he failed to satisfy the requirements for executorship in Iowa and thus never took part in the will proceedings. Instead, Alexander Sanford, Irene's father, was appointed, and when he died in 1848 no successor was named. Even though John Sanford was later involved in the trial, there is no known legal connection between him and Emerson's will. When the estate was settled, Irene Emerson had full control of her husband's property.

Slaves belonging to Emerson were not mentioned in the will. For the next three years after his death, his wife hired out the Scotts. Scott apparently spent most of that time with Irene's brother-in-law, Captain Henry Bainbridge. He was probably with Bainbridge at Fort Jesup in 1844 and went with him the following year to the newly annexed state of Texas. However, Scott's wife and daughters may have stayed in St. Louis. The couple's second daughter, Lizzie, was born in 1846 at Jefferson Barracks in St. Louis.

Scott was sent back to St. Louis, probably at Irene Emerson's request, in February 1846. He and his wife were hired out to a local man named Samuel Russell. Shortly after his return, Scott tried to buy his family's freedom with a partial payment of $300, and security for the remainder. However, according to Scott's later testimony, Irene Emerson refused the request, and therefore, on April 6, 1846, Dred and Harriet Scott filed petitions in the Missouri Circuit Court of St. Louis. They petitioned to sue for their freedom and that of their two daughters.

## THe FIrST STeP DOWN THe ROaD

Why would an illiterate slave suddenly sue for freedom when he had not seemed to be aware of his condition during the time he lived in free territory? No one knows for sure. One possibility is simply that Scott himself finally thought of the idea. He may have learned about such matters during his travels with Emerson. Any number of people may have told him of the possibilities for freedom under the law. As for expenses, so many lawyers became involved that it is likely their services were donated or very cheap. Although John Emerson himself might have promised Scott his freedom, such a promise would have been useless to Scott because the will did not mention him. Some experts suggest that Taylor Blow or someone else in his family may have discussed freedom with their former slave.

In addition, Harriet Scott had joined the Second

African Baptist Church in St. Louis. The reverend, John R. Anderson, had been a slave himself but had bought his freedom and he may have told Harriet Scott that she was legally entitled to hers. A unique reason for the suit was voiced in 1907 by a lawyer, Frederick Trevor Hill, who argued that, "although the motive for the case ostensibly was to secure freedom by 'testing' the laws on slavery, the real reason was to pave the way for a second suit against the Emerson estate for back wages to which Scott would be entitled once the court found that he had been held illegally as a slave." Historians, however, say such a theory is not supported by any facts.

Whatever the reason or reasons, there is no evidence to suggest that the case began for political gain or because someone talked Scott into a test case. Scott himself supposedly said that he "never understood 'all the fuss they made' over his case. He only wanted his freedom." In the end, perhaps it was that simple.

The Scotts' lawyer, Francis B. Murdoch, filed two suits against Irene Emerson: *Dred Scott* v. *Irene Emerson* and *Harriet Scott* v. *Irene Emerson*. They both cited trespass and false imprisonment. This was the type of charge that the law required slaves to use when petitioning for their freedom. Claiming that they were free persons, the Scotts charged that Irene Emerson had assaulted them and made them prisoners without any reasonable cause.

Only the Dred Scott case continued through the courts since it was decided that the outcome for Scott would cover Harriet as well. The two suits were not precisely the same, however, since Harriet had never lived in the free state of Illinois.

# First Lawyer For The Plaintiff

Dred Scott's first lawyer was Francis B. Murdoch, something of a mystery man. No one knows exactly how he came to file the Scott petition. He was known to be against slavery but did not regularly handle slave cases. He had, however, been an attorney in Alton, Illinois, in 1837 when Elijah P. Lovejoy, an antislavery newspaper publisher, was writing strong editorial condemnations of slavery. After many threats and much violence, Lovejoy was killed by a rioting mob that destroyed his printing presses.

Also in Alton at the time was Reverend John R. Anderson, who later became pastor of the Second African Baptist Church in St. Louis, which Harriet Scott attended. Thus, it is possible that Anderson and Murdoch became acquainted, either in Alton or St. Louis, and that Murdoch was persuaded to file the first petition. Interestingly enough, for reasons that were never known, he left St. Louis before the case even came to trial.

Irene Emerson answered with pleas of not guilty to both suits. Her response was filed on November 19, 1846. Because of a very crowded court schedule—a condition still common in the twenty-first century—the suits did not come to trial until June 30, 1847. However, the verdict was returned that same day.

## THE TRIAL AND VERDICT

To use a term from basketball, most of those involved with Dred Scott regarded his suit as a slam dunk. The slave and his wife would soon be free. There were many legal precedents for assuming their freedom. In 1824 the Missouri Supreme Court, in *Vinny* v. *Whitesides*, declared a slave free because he had been taken to Illinois. In little more than a decade, the Missouri court decided the same way in ten other cases. Always the deciding factor was showing that the former slave had been in free territory long enough to be called a resident. Other slave states, such as Kentucky, Mississippi, and Louisiana, made similar decisions.

All these rulings stemmed from *Somerset* v. *Stewart* (1772) in Great Britain. The English high court had ruled that slavery itself was so contrary to natural law, so odious, that only the passing of specific laws could support the institution. Therefore, once a slave was taken into territory that had no laws supporting slavery, the slave was a free person—and once a free person, he or she remained a free person. From the Somerset ruling came the concept of "once free, always free."

On trial day in June 1847, Alexander Hamilton (not the famous political figure of the nation's founding period) was the presiding judge. He was a Philadelphia native and although new on the bench, his sympathy toward freedom suits was well known. Scott's lawyers were pleased that

18

An article in *Frank Leslie's Illustrated Newspaper* recounts a visit to Dred Scott, with illustrations of him and his family.

# Harriet Scott, wife of a slave

After Harriet and her husband were given their freedom, the Scotts were convinced by *Frank Leslie's Illustrated Newspaper* to have their photograph, called a daguerreotype, taken. Harriet refused at first because she had heard that many people would be trying to make money off their newfound publicity. When she was assured that the paper had no such intentions, she agreed. As a result, the Scotts, including their two daughters, were photographed by a well-known St. Louis photographer, J. H. Fitzgibbons. The only known portraits of the family appeared in the June 27, 1857, issue of the paper. The picture of Scott that is used in most history books was taken from a painting that was copied from the original photograph.

Details of what happened to the Scott family after his death are vague. It is thought that Harriet and Eliza lived only a few years longer and Lizzie married a man named Wilson Madison of St. Louis and had two sons.

Hamilton had recently replaced the proslavery advocate Judge John Krum on the bench. A Virginian, George W. Goode, a proslavery lawyer, represented Irene Emerson. Murdoch, Scott's lawyer, had moved away from St. Louis and was replaced by former Missouri attorney general Samuel M. Bay. The Blow family took on Scott's expenses. The trial took place in what is now called the Old Courthouse in St. Louis, a national historic landmark, that at the time was not fully completed.

Bay had only to show that Scott had been taken to live on free soil and that he was at present a slave held by Irene Emerson. Obviously the first point was easy to prove with accounts taken from soldiers at Fort Snelling. However, surprisingly, there was trouble with the second. Samuel Russell, who was called upon to testify that he had hired the Scotts from Emerson, under cross-examination admitted that his wife had done the hiring and that he had paid the money to Irene Emerson's father, Alexander Sanford. Samuel Russell assumed that the money was for Irene Emerson, but he did not know it for sure. And that was the problem, strange as it seems. Everyone knew that Dred Scott and his wife were Irene Emerson's slaves. But no one seemed to know how to prove it.

The verdict was quickly handed down. The Scotts lost. Irene Emerson was entitled to keep her slaves simply because no one could prove that they *were* her slaves. The Scotts had waited a year to be denied freedom on a technicality.

## THE FIRST APPEAL

On the day after the decision, Scott's lawyers filed a petition for a new suit. They argued that they had been

PERMISSION FOR DRED SCOTT TO SUE FOR FREEDOM IS GRANTED BY
JUDGE JOHN KRUM, CIRCUIT COURT OF ST. LOUIS COUNTY, ON
APRIL 6, 1848.

unprepared for Russell's testimony and that the fact in dispute—Emerson's ownership of the Scotts—could be readily established. Not wanting to leave any loopholes in the case, they also filed petitions against Alexander Sanford and Samuel Russell in addition to Emerson. However, a month later Judge Hamilton ruled that the Scotts had to decide on one suit only, against Sanford, Russell, and Emerson, or against Emerson. They chose to file against Emerson.

Interestingly, during this period the Scotts had been working for Russell and hired out to others. Emerson's lawyer requested and was granted a motion that the sheriff take charge of hiring out the Scotts during the trial period. In effect, Irene Emerson was now relieved of the responsibility for the slaves but did not give up her claim to them.

The lawyers may have been quick to file, but fixing the trial date was a far less speedy matter. It was not until January 12, 1850, more than a year and a half after the original trial, that the Scotts were once again in court. Beyond the usual backup in the legal system, part of the reason for the long delay was a major fire and a cholera epidemic in the city.

By now Scott was being represented by Alexander P. Field, an expert trial lawyer, and David N. Hall. Emerson had replaced Goode with Hugh A. Garland and Lyman D. Norris. This time, Field included testimony from Mrs. Russell that she had indeed hired the Scotts from Emerson. This time, the jury decided in the Scotts' favor.

After four years in the courts, the slave Dred Scott was a free man. But not for long. A subtle change was taking place. It seemed that, as determined as Dred Scott was to win his freedom, so was Irene Emerson determined to keep him a slave. It has been suggested that this determination stemmed from bitterness between Emerson and the Blow family, which was paying the costs of Scott's suit. Some speculate that Emerson had actually sold the Scotts to her brother and that he was merely protecting his own investment. Whatever the reason, attorneys for Emerson appealed the decision to the Missouri Supreme Court. That appeal, too, seemed odd since Missouri's highest court had time and again decided that a slave residing in a free state was a free person.

It took another two years for Dred Scott to have another day in court. By that time, Irene Emerson was not even in St. Louis. She had moved to Springfield, Massachusetts, in late 1849 and the following year married another doctor, an antislavery advocate named Calvin C. Chaffee, who later became a congressman. Back in Missouri, Emerson's brother, John Sanford, acted on her behalf in the Scott case. Because a reporter at the state supreme court misspelled Sanford's name, the case went into the legal files and into the history books as *Scott* v. *Sandford*.

Until this time, the *Dred Scott* case had attracted little attention outside the circle of those who were directly involved. Although it still seemed as though Scott would win, either way, the trial did not involve any particular political implications. However, slowly through the years, especially the years while all these legal proceedings were crawling through the courts, the political atmosphere had indeed been changing. It was changing step by step, argument by argument, law by law, and bitterness by bitterness. The United States was coming apart over the issue of slavery. In that time and in that place, Dred Scott, the slave, would soon find himself right in the middle of a larger and very critical controversy.

Slaves were essential to the profitable tobacco trade in the South.

# TWO
# THE WAY IT WAS

DURING THE FIRST HALF of the nineteenth century, the United States was increasingly preoccupied with the institution of slavery. It was part of everyday life everywhere. Northerners sneered at southerners for their treatment of blacks, even while often confining dark-skinned people to ghettos in northern cities. Southerners, most of whom could not afford to own slaves in the first place, defended the institution fiercely. Every issue in Congress seemed to wind up with accusations that involved blacks and their place in America.

## THE BEGINNINGS
The slavery issue had taken a long time to come to a boil. The first blacks in North America were Africans who were brought on a Dutch ship to the British colony at Jamestown, Virginia, in 1619. Over the next several decades, more blacks arrived and were introduced into the other colonies. Others came as indentured servants, white and black; they served for a specified number of years and then were given freedom. By the middle of the seventeenth century, however, indentured servitude was at an end for blacks, who became slaves. White servants were generally allowed to work off their terms. So slavery became a matter of race.

As the colonies prospered, the English colonists developed plantations to produce cotton, tobacco, and sugar, and more and more slaves were needed to work the fields. Slave trading soon became more profitable than growing crops. Thus, the so-called triangle trade developed. There was more than one arrangement, but the most famous involved New Englanders trading basic manufactured goods for slaves in West Africa. The slaves were brought to the West Indies, where they were traded for rum and molasses to be sold in North America. By the late 1600s, there were only about two thousand slaves in the colonies. By 1750 there were 236,400 slaves, all but 30,400 of whom lived south of Pennsylvania. By Dred Scott's time in the mid-nineteenth century, there were more than four million.

A slave was a piece of property to be bought or sold at the owner's will. The slave was in most respects treated like a domestic animal, worked to whatever degree in whatever labor the owner saw fit. Any children of the slave became the property of the slave's owner. When a child was born of both slave and free parents, if the mother was a slave, as was usually the case, the infant was a slave. Slaves in the South could not own property or testify against a white person in court. In short, a slave had no rights. Slave treatment in the North was generally more lenient than in the South, where there were far more slaves and owners were more afraid of rebellion. It was assumed that slaves required constant supervision and restraint.

By the early 1700s, the colonies had passed slave codes to define and regulate slavery. According to the slave codes, slavery was both lifelong and hereditary, passed on from slave to slave.

# slave code of virginia

Although the details of his early years are very vague, Dred Scott was probably born in Virginia around 1800. Therefore, he would have been subject to the slave code of the Virginia General Assembly, which in 1705 declared that slaves were to be regarded as property. Thus, if any slave required punishment that happened to result in his or her death, the owner or master was free of any punishment.

The slave code of Virginia became a model for the other colonies. Punishment for infractions was always physical since someone who did not own property could not be expected to pay a fine. Slaves had to have written permission to leave their plantations. For a major offense such as murder, a slave was hanged. For robbery the slave would get sixty lashes and placement in the stocks, where his or her ears were cut off. For a minor offense, such as talking without permission to a white person, the slave would be whipped or perhaps maimed in some way or branded as an offender.

Before the slave code of Virginia was enacted in 1705, slave and master could be brought before a court for judgment over a dispute. After 1705, slave owners had absolute control over their slaves and did not have to answer to the law for how they treated them.

In the seventeenth and eighteenth centuries, an intellectual movement called the Enlightenment swept through Europe. Influential leaders were inspired by faith in the possibility of a better world and began to build programs of reform in politics, art, and philosophy. Enlightenment leaders claimed that the goals of a rational being were knowledge, happiness, and freedom. For many, these goals implied a hatred of slavery. Societies were formed both in Britain and the United States to end the slave trade. England abolished the slave trade in 1807 and by 1833 the slaves in their West Indies colonies were free. It took a civil war and the Thirteenth Amendment to the Constitution to end slavery in the United States in 1865. Slavery is no longer recognized legally anywhere in the world; the last nation to abolish it officially was the northwest African country of Mauritania, in 1980.

## IN THE MIDST OF THE STORM

By the time the *Dred Scott* case reached the Missouri Supreme Court, the nation was in a fury over slavery. Lawmakers thought they had settled the thorny slavery issue back in 1820 when they passed the Missouri Compromise. Actually, the compromise turned out to be only the beginning of a prolonged conflict.

The Missouri Territory had first applied for statehood in 1817. Two years later Congress was about to pass legislation to frame a state constitution when Senator James Tallmadge of New York insisted that an antislavery amendment be added. The amendment forbade any more slaves from entering Missouri and freed slaves already there when they reached the age of twenty-five. It passed in the House but failed in the Senate before Congress adjourned.

When Congress reconvened in December 1819,

Maine also requested statehood. Illinois Senator Jesse B. Thomas then added an amendment allowing Missouri to enter the Union as a slave state but forbidding slavery in the rest of the Louisiana Territory north of latitutde 36° 30', which was Missouri's southern border.

The so-called Missouri Compromise of 1820 was passed on March 3 with the help of Senator Henry Clay of Kentucky. Maine was admitted as the twenty-third state on March 15, and Missouri was authorized to adopt a state constitution with no restrictions on slavery.

Almost immediately there was a new crisis. The Missouri constitutional convention gave the new state legislature the right to exclude free blacks and people of mixed parentage. Clay stepped in again. The Second Missouri Compromise of March 2, 1821, said that Missouri could not become a state if it abridged the privileges and immunities of U.S. citizens. Missouri agreed, but as history shows, that was only the beginning of the trouble. It became the twenty-fourth state on August 10, 1821.

The country now had one new free state, one new slave state, and free territory in all western land north of Missouri's southern border. The Missouri Compromise was viewed as a hope for peace because it maintained the balance between free states and slave states in the Union. However, several events that followed only increased friction on both sides. It was Scott's misfortune to have his case judged in the legal system when the political atmosphere so greatly influenced the Missouri court's decision.

In 1850 the U.S. Congress passed another law in its futile attempt to ward off civil war over the issue of slavery. The Compromise of 1850 resulted from California's request the preceding year to enter the

Union as a free state. The Mexican-American War, which ended in 1848, had enlarged the United States by more than 500,000 square miles, from the Rio Grande to the Pacific Ocean. Pennsylvania Congressman David Wilmot introduced an amendment forbidding slavery in the new territory. A bitter debate raged, but the so-called Wilmot Proviso never passed. California's request opened up that argument once again.

This request might possibly have brought on war but for Senator Henry Clay of Kentucky, known as the Great Compromiser. With his efforts, a compromise was reached. California would enter as a free state, New Mexico and Utah would be organized as territories, with the slavery question left open—once again a temporary solution. (The New Mexico territory included the present-day states of New Mexico and Arizona and part of Colorado; the Utah territory included present-day Utah and Nevada.) In addition, the boundary between the United States and Mexico would be settled, the slave trade would be banned in the District of Columbia, and a new law would be passed for the return of runaway slaves. It was hoped that this new salve, the Compromise of 1850, would settle tempers on both sides.

However, the law passed for the return of runaway slaves, the Fugitive Slave Act of 1850, only caused further outrage in the North. In fact, it led to more trouble than perhaps any other previous legislation. The act provided for the seizure and return of slaves who had escaped from one state to another or into federal territory. A similar law passed in 1793 had proved ineffective. Since that time, various stratagems, such as the Underground Railroad, a secret escape route to help slaves to freedom in the North or Canada, had increased the number of runaways.

# THE Underground Railroad: Another Way to Freedom

While Dred Scott was seeking freedom in a law court, thousands of slaves were taking a more desperate, if shorter, route. The Underground Railroad, neither underground nor a railroad, was a system that existed in the northern states before the Civil War to help slaves escape to freedom in the North or Canada. It was so named because activity had to be carried out in darkness and because railroad terms were used. Stopping-off places were called "stations," people who helped the slaves were known as "conductors," and the runaway slaves themselves were called "freight" or "packages."

Routes on the railroad extended in all directions throughout fourteen northern states and Canada. Northern abolitionists and philanthropists greatly assisted the work of the railroad but none so much as a group of free blacks, which included Harriet Tubman and other former slaves. The actual number of white northerners who participated in the running of this escape system was small. However, the Underground Railroad did much to gain sympathy from the North for the plight of the slaves. During the period before the Civil War, anywhere from 60,000 to 75,000 slaves were said to have escaped to freedom in the North.

In an effort to stop escaping slaves, the South demanded harsher, more effective laws. Congress, still trying to close the open slavery wound, responded with the Fugitive Slave Act. Heavy penalties were imposed on marshals who refused to enforce the law and on anyone helping a slave escape. If caught, the escaped slave had no right to a trial and could not testify on his or her own behalf.

The new act was so severe that it defeated its own purpose. The Underground Railroad merely became more secretive and more efficient. Personal-liberty laws were passed in many northern states. These laws guaranteed fugitive slaves a trial by jury, a right denied them by the new act. And the number of abolitionists, those working for the end of slavery, vastly increased. The law would not be repealed until 1864.

## missouri in the middle

Both sides in the *Dred Scott* case filed their briefs with the Missouri Supreme Court on March 8, 1850. (It was at this point that the court reporter misspelled Sanford's name as Sandford.) Once again, the wheels of justice moved slowly; the decision was not handed down until two years later.

The original suit filed on behalf of Scott and his wife had begun in April 1846. Much had changed in the mood of the country—and of Missouri—since that time. The North was upset over the Fugitive Slave Act. The South was growing more resentful about the constant attacks on its culture. More and more, attempts to pass antislavery laws such as the Wilmot Proviso seemed an attack on the southern way of life. Increasingly, editorials in northern newspapers and church sermons railed against slavery and those who practiced it. As a result, the South became ever more grimly determined to stand its ground.

DEPARTURE OF BRIG ACORN WITH SIMS ON BOARD.

THE FUGITIVE SLAVE ACT MADE IT ILLEGAL TO HELP AN ESCAPED
SLAVE TO FREEDOM, BUT MANY IN THE NORTH IGNORED THE LAW.
THEY DID EVERYTHING THEY COULD TO HELP RESCUE ESCAPED SLAVES,
SUCH AS THE SLAVE NAMED SIMS MENTIONED IN THIS ETCHING.

# 135,000 SETS, 270,000 VOLUMES SOLD.

# UNCLE TOM'S CABIN

# FOR SALE HERE.

AN EDITION FOR THE MILLION, COMPLETE IN 1 Vol., PRICE 37 1-2 CENTS.

" " IN GERMAN, IN 1 Vol., PRICE 50 CENTS.

" " IN 2 Vols,. CLOTH, 6 PLATES, PRICE $1.50.

SUPERB ILLUSTRATED EDITION, IN 1 Vol., WITH 153 ENGRAVINGS,

PRICES FROM $2.50 TO $5.00.

# The Greatest Book of the Age.

UNCLE TOM'S CABIN; OR, LIFE AMONG THE LOWLY, A NOVEL WRITTEN BY HARRIET BEECHER STOWE, INFLUENCED FEELINGS AGAINST SLAVERY SO MUCH IT HAS SOMETIMES BEEN CITED AS A CAUSE OF THE CIVIL WAR. PUBLISHED IN 1852, THE BOOK HAS NEVER GONE OUT OF PRINT.

# THe BOOK THaT caused a war

The atmosphere in which the Missouri Supreme Court deliberated on Scott's freedom was further inflamed in 1852 by the publication of a book, *Uncle Tom's Cabin; or, Life Among the Lowly*. It had appeared as a serial the year before in the *National Era*, an antislavery paper in Washington, D.C. Written by Harriet Beecher Stowe, daughter of a Congregationalist minister, the book contributed so much to popular feelings against slavery that it is sometimes cited as one of the causes of the American Civil War. It is said that Abraham Lincoln met the author sometime after the book's publication and referred to her as the little lady who started a war.

About half of the novel focuses on the slave Eliza and her son, who escape to freedom across the Ohio River. The story struck a chord with northerners. Stowe herself had lived for eighteen years in Cincinnati. There, she came in contact with fugitive slaves crossing the Ohio from a slave-holding community. She also visited the South and learned about life in the slaveholding states from the stories of friends. When Stowe and her husband, a clergyman and professor, moved to Brunswick, Maine, in 1850, she wrote her famous novel. Before long her name was a symbol of hatred in the South. However, the book enjoyed great popularity elsewhere. It was translated into more than twenty languages and made into a play. In the year 1853, Stowe published *The Key to Uncle Tom's Cabin*, which presented many documents and testimonies against slavery. The author died in Hartford, Connecticut, in 1896.

In the middle of this groundswell, both geographically and historically, stood Missouri. Having been a focal point of the Missouri Compromise, it was especially sensitive to the subject of slavery. Three of its borders faced free territory. Unlike the other slave states, Missouri contained a very vocal antislavery group. Its membership may have been a minority, but it was certainly visible and intimidated the state's slave owners or, at the least, made them uncomfortable. Also, Missouri's longtime Democratic leader, Senator Thomas Hart Benton, had made many enemies, even in his own party, because of his moderate views on slavery, among other things. For all these reasons, neither the state nor the Missouri Supreme Court was the same in 1852 as it had been four years earlier.

## strader v. Graham

Another Supreme Court case that would have some bearing on the Missouri decision was *Strader* v. *Graham* (1851). The case involved some Kentucky slave musicians who had performed briefly in the free states of Ohio and Indiana and later escaped from Kentucky into Canada. The suit was filed by the owner against those who had helped the slaves escape. The defense argued that the slaves were free once they stepped on Ohio and Indiana soil because of the Northwest Ordinance of 1787. This law laid the basis for governing the Northwest Territory and forever outlawed slavery there. Therefore, the slaves ran off to Canada as free men, not slaves. However, the Kentucky Court of Appeals rejected this argument and ruled in favor of the slave owner. The matter was then sent to the U.S. Supreme Court.

Kentucky argued that it did not matter if the slaves

were free when they were in Ohio and Indiana. Once back in Kentucky, they were slaves again. Chief Justice Roger Taney (pronounced "Tawney") also said that the Northwest Ordinance did not apply in this case anyway because Ohio and Indiana were now states, not territories.

Taney, who would write the Court's decision in the *Dred Scott* case, voiced the unanimous opinion in *Strader v. Graham*. He declared that the highest court had no jurisdiction to rule. The status of the slaves had to be decided by the Kentucky court. As stated by Kermit Hall in *The Oxford Companion to the Supreme Court of the United States*, "Thus it was up to each state to determine for itself the status of persons within its jurisdiction, and this was not subject to review by the Supreme Court. *Strader* left it for each state, and an issue of interstate comity, to decide if a slave gained freedom through residence or sojourn in a free state." (Interstate comity refers to a state recognizing the laws and judicial decisions of another state.)

## slave again?
The supreme court of Missouri consisted of three justices. Only one, Hamilton R. Gamble, was antislavery. The other two were William Scott and John F. Ryland. The court met on October 20, 1851, and almost postponed the case again. However, at the last minute Alexander Field was able to get it on the court calendar. He was now Scott's only lawyer, David Hall having died. Field resubmitted the same briefs that had been filed in 1850. Lyman Norris, one of Emerson's attorneys, was working on a new brief when he found out that the case had been turned over to Judge William Scott for the opinion of the court. This assignment was an obvious

indication of where the verdict was going since Judge Scott was known to be avidly proslavery.

The indications were correct, for on March 22, 1852, the Missouri Supreme Court gave its ruling. Dred Scott would remain a slave; the decision of the lower court was reversed, as were nearly three decades of favorable decisions on the slavery issue in Missouri. Justice William Scott read the court's opinion. He acknowledged that in other similar cases, slaves were given freedom because they had lived in free territory. He said those cases had been decided on grounds of interstate comity obligating Missouri to enforce the laws of other states. However, Scott said Missouri courts did not have to recognize laws of other states when they interfered with Missouri's own laws.

The Missouri court's decision was openly political, reflecting the increasing sentiment in the South. Said Justice Scott,

> Times are not now as they were when the former decisions on this subject were made. Since then, not only individuals but States have been possessed with a dark and fell spirit in relation to slavery, whose gratification is sought in the pursuit of measures, whose inevitable consequence must be the overthrow and destruction of our Government. Under such circumstances, it does not behoove the State of Missouri to show the least countenance to any measure which might gratify this spirit. She is willing to assume her full responsibility for the existence of slavery within her limits, nor does she seek to share or divide it with others.

Then for good measure, he added the following: "We are almost persuaded that the introduction of slavery amongst us was, in the providence of God, who makes the evil passions of men subservient to His own glory, a means of placing that unhappy race within the pale of civilized nations."

Even though there was now no need for Lyman Norris to complete his brief since the case had already been turned over to the court, he filed it anyway because he wanted some of his political thoughts to be heard. He stated the belief of many that the North was trying to destroy the southern way of life by ending slavery. He said that Missouri had the right to decide whether or not to uphold the laws of another state. He also claimed that neither the Northwest Ordinance nor the Missouri Compromise had any authority and so could not be enforced—an eerie hint of the final U.S. Supreme Court decision.

Hamilton Gamble, the lone antislavery judge on the court, wrote a dissenting opinion. His basic argument was that the court had not voted on the individual in the case. The decision of his two colleagues, Gamble said, was the result of their anger over the slavery question and not of careful consideration of the facts. In other words, according to Gamble, the court was using Dred Scott to fight back against all the growing antislavery sentiment of the past years.

Six years had passed since Dred Scott had asked for his freedom, and he was still a slave. This time, however, it seemed that the matter was settled. Surely, Irene Emerson and John Sanford thought so. Nothing in the case of Dred Scott ever went entirely according to plan, however, and this time was no exception.

## to the federal courts

After the Missouri court ruling in March, Emerson's lawyers filed a motion that called for ending the sheriff's custody of Scott, which had been in effect for about four years. Since Scott and his wife had been hired out during this period, Emerson demanded payment of what they had earned during that time. The sheriff had been collecting the money and holding it in the bank until the case was settled. By now a substantial sum had been collected.

Judge Hamilton denied Emerson's petition. He also put off what should have been a formality—carrying out the decision of the higher court; that is, returning Scott and his wife to the ownership of Emerson. Instead, they were ordered to be kept in custody by the sheriff. It is unclear why Hamilton acted in this way, except that he might have already been told that Scott's lawyer was going to appeal to the U.S. Supreme Court. However, the appeal did not happen immediately.

The delay might have occurred because Scott was without a lawyer again. Alexander Field moved to Louisiana and could no longer represent him. Two years after Scott was placed in custody, he was hired by Charles LaBeaume, brother-in-law to one of the Blow sons. The family was still backing the Scott case, and it is believed that Scott continued to work for LaBeaume as long as the trials went on.

LaBeaume, himself a lawyer, now asked for the aid of Roswell Field (no relation to Scott's previous attorney, Alexander Field). Field had a considerable reputation as a strong antislavery lawyer. It is obvious that the Blow family was determined to win.

Field did not appeal the trial decision directly to the

WHEN SCOTT WAS LEFT WITHOUT LEGAL COUNSEL, LAWYER ROSWELL FIELD AGREED TO WORK FREE OF CHARGE. HE FILED SUIT AGAINST SCOTT'S ALLEGED OWNER, JOHN SANFORD, FOR BATTERY AND WRONGFUL IMPRISONMENT.

U.S. Supreme Court, contrary to standard procedure, because he believed that action was useless. At the time, the only ground for such an appeal was that the Missouri court had made an error in its decision. Field believed that the high court would simply refuse to review the case, just as it had done with *Strader* v. *Graham*.

Instead, Field entered a suit in the U.S. Circuit Court against John Sanford, whether he was acting as Scott's owner or Emerson's representative. Sanford later declared that Emerson, who by now had married Chaffee, had sold Scott to him. However, no bill of sale was ever found. When Sanford died in 1857, the Scotts were not mentioned in his will, and when Taylor Blow bought the Scotts after Sanford's death, he did so from the Chaffee family, not the Sanfords.

The suit was filed on November 2, 1853, and was heard the following April in the St. Louis federal circuit court. John Sanford, who by this time had moved to New York, was charged with battery and wrongful imprisonment. The presiding judge was Robert W. Wells, a slave owner who nevertheless had doubts about how far the South could progress as long as slavery was part of its everyday institutions.

The new suit charged Sanford, a citizen of New York, with illegally holding Scott, a citizen of Missouri, as a slave. But before the trial began, Sanford filed a plea stating that the court had no jurisdiction to hear the case because Scott was not a citizen of Missouri. Scott was not a citizen of the state of Missouri, declared Sanford, "because he is a negro of African descent; his ancestors were of pure African blood, and were brought into this country and sold as negro slaves." In other words, Sanford claimed that no black person, slave or free, could be a citizen of the state of Missouri.

Wells rejected Sanford's challenge. He said that Scott had the right to sue. He did not say that Scott, even as a free man, was entitled to full equality, but he did believe that the word *citizen* referred to a resident of a state. So if Dred Scott was not a slave, he indeed met the requirements to be a citizen of Missouri.

Sanford also had to respond in court to Scott's charges of physically mistreating him. He did not deny doing so but declared that he was within his rights because he owned Scott. Sanford believed he had a right to restrain Scott since he was a slave.

The trial date was May 15, 1854. Interestingly, at this time the Kansas-Nebraska bill was fighting its way through Congress. It provided for the organization of the two new territories, and it became law on May 30. (The Kansas Territory conforms to the present state of Kansas. But the Nebraska Territory was five times larger than Nebraska is today. In addition to the present state of Nebraska, it included the present-day states of North Dakota, South Dakota, and parts of Montana, Wyoming, and Colorado.) The Missouri Compromise of 1820 had banned slavery from all land in the Louisiana Purchase north of 36° 30', except for Missouri. The Kansas-Nebraska Act violated the Missouri Compromise by saying that the question of slavery in the two territories was to be decided by the voters. This became known as the doctrine of popular sovereignty. The Compromise of 1850 concerning the territories of New Mexico and Utah had also left the issue of slavery up to the people.

Although the Kansas-Nebraska Act was intended to stop the growing friction over extending slavery, it made the situation worse. Antislavery people were furious. Disagreement over the issue became so heated in the Kansas Territory that it erupted into an intense period of bloodshed and political chaos known as "Bleeding Kansas."

No new witnesses were called at the trial of Dred Scott, and no new evidence was introduced. Field asked Judge Wells to instruct the jury to free Scott according to the Northwest Ordinance, the Missouri Compromise, and the laws of Illinois. Wells said no. Instead he agreed with the Missouri Supreme Court that Scott had to be tried under the laws of Missouri, not Illinois. Since Missouri had already decided that Scott was a slave, a slave he would remain. Wells later said that he wished the law had been on the side of Scott but that under the law he had no other choice.

RUINS OF THE FREE STATE HOTEL, LAWRENCE.
From the Daguerreotype taken for Mrs Robinson.

LAWRENCE, KANSAS, WAS FOUNDED BY ANTISLAVERY ADVOCATES BENT ON MAKING
KANSAS A NONSLAVE STATE. SHORTLY AFTERWARD, THE HOTEL AND NEWSPAPER
OFFICE WERE BURNT DOWN BY PROSLAVERY ADVOCATES.

# "BLEEDING KANSAS"

During the years 1854–1859, a small civil war erupted between proslavery and antislavery advocates for control of the new territory of Kansas. Sponsors of the Kansas-Nebraska Act of 1854, which said that voters would decide the slavery issue in each territory, had expected its passage to stop the fanaticism that was dividing the country. The opposite occurred. Associations and guerrilla bands formed on each side of the issue, and advocates began to pour into the territory. When an antislavery settler was murdered in December 1855, only the interference of the territorial governor prevented all-out violence.

In 1856, "Bleeding Kansas" became a reality. The town of Lawrence had been founded two years earlier by antislavery radicals intent on outvoting the proslavery faction and making Kansas a free state. It was named for a New England textile manufacturer named Amos Lawrence, who had helped promote the town's settlement by abolitionists. Lawrence became a noted station on the Underground Railroad and headquarters for the abolitionists. On May 21 a proslavery militia led by David Rice Atchison, a former Democratic senator from Missouri, sacked the town and burned the hotel and newspaper office, claiming it was a hotbed of abolitionism.

Periodic bloodshed followed, and the chaos was not ended until 1861, when Kansas was admitted to the Union as a free state. However, the term "Bleeding Kansas" had furnished the newly formed Republican Party with what turned out to be a successful antislavery issue in the national election of 1860. In 1863, the town was attacked again, this time by Confederate guerrilla William Clarke Quantrill and his raiders. They killed one hundred fifty citizens.

Sanford was found not guilty of the charges. Dred Scott was still a slave. The principle of "once free, always free" was gone. Roswell Field immediately called for a new trial and was denied. The next stop was the Supreme Court of the United States.

This step was not to be taken lightly. For one thing, appealing to the nation's highest court was expensive. Legal costs would be far more than the Blow family, which had long been Scott's backers, could afford. So they either had to raise the money for his defense or find a lawyer who would take the case for free.

Surprisingly perhaps, considering the atmosphere of the time, Dred Scott's quest for freedom had so far attracted little public attention. The St. Louis *Herald* carried a small article with this sentiment: "Dred is, of course, poor and without any powerful friends. But no doubt he will find at the bar of the Supreme Court some able and generous advocate, who will do all he can to establish his right to go free."

That result is what the Blow family also wanted. Scott's present lawyer, Roswell Field, had no experience before the U.S. Supreme Court. To raise money for an experienced lawyer, Charles LaBeaume published a twelve-page pamphlet describing the recent trial.

A short preface was written as though by Scott himself and dated July 4 for emotional effect. It ended with a personal appeal for help: "I have no money to pay anybody at Washington to speak for me. My fellow-men, can any of you help me in my day of trial? Will nobody speak for me at Washington, even without hope of other reward than the blessings of a poor black man and his family?" It was signed with Scott's mark.

Apparently, no one could help in Scott's day of trial, or no one wanted to. The lack of response seems

# FRANK LESLIE'S
# ILLUSTRATED

# NEWSPAPER

No. 40.—VOL. II.]      NEW YORK, SATURDAY, SEPTEMBER 13, 1856.      [PRICE TEN CENTS.

## REMOVAL OF THE QUARANTINE.

It is now universally conceded that the Quarantine must be removed. The universal popular voice must be obeyed. It has spoken loudly and long, hitherto without any decided effect; but recent events have aroused a sentiment and created an excitement, which will not be allayed, until some determined, positive, and efficient action shall have been taken. Years since, the legislature of this State passed an enactment in favor of a removal to Sandy Hook, and the consent of the United States authorities at Washington was obtained. But this enactment was rendered nugatory at the time in consequence of the objection and opposition of the State of New Jersey, which claimed a kind of jurisdiction over the land at Sandy Hook. Notwithstanding the ownership of this property is in the United States, this objection has hitherto prevailed—an objection founded on the assumption, that, in the cession by New Jersey of this territory to the United States, it was made for a specific purpose, namely, that of the erection of a light-house.

But, even if we yield full weight to this objection, this surely is a case in which comity between the States should incline New Jersey to act as if her own interests were identical with those of New York. The truth is, the inhabitants of a considerable and important portion of New Jersey are as much interested in the speedy and final removal of the "Quarantine" from its present neighborhood, as are the citizens of Manhattan Island, Long Island, and Staten Island. A virulent epidemic, originating in ships from foreign ports, if conveyed to the great cities of Brooklyn and New York, would infallibly reach Jersey City, and perform its mission of destruction with equal power through all our borders. Such a consideration should, and doubtless will, have a conclusive influence, and the day is not distant when both shores of the Hudson River will unite in fervent congratulations on the improved condition of the public health — a condition brought about by the more distant location of a grand and fertile source of disease.

After the removal of the Marine Hospital shall have taken place, the wonder then will be universal that this community should so long have submitted to the existence of a Lazaretto, or pest-house, in the very midst of a dense population. The reasons for this removal, *at any expense and with any conceivable sacrifice in the shortest possible time*, are so numerous and obvious that it is unnecessary to recapitulate them all, or even a majority of them. The chief reason, of course, is that it furnishes a potent and probable cause of sickness. Its accessibility is such that, in spite of all precautions and prohibitions, the Quarantine may be broken, and infected persons find their way into the city. This is frequently done, and has been done within the last few weeks, so that were Yellow Fever communicable from one to another, as the contagionists would have us believe, the

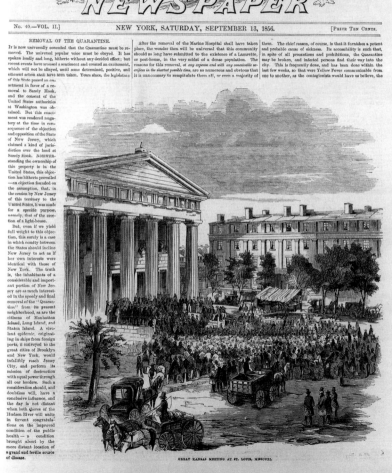

GREAT KANSAS MEETING AT ST. LOUIS, MISSOURI.

SLAVERY WAS A HOTLY DEBATED ISSUE IN KANSAS, WHERE ADVOCATES ON BOTH SIDES WERE FIERCE AND COULD BE VIOLENT.

strange, especially from the normally vocal antislavery group. Perhaps the abolitionists were too busy fighting their own battles to realize as yet the importance—and the significance—of one case involving an illiterate black man.

Months went by and still no lawyer came forward for Scott. Finally, on Christmas Eve 1854, Roswell Field contacted a prominent Washington attorney named Montgomery Blair. He had approached Blair months earlier about taking the case without pay. This time, after talking the matter over with his family and friends, Blair agreed on the condition that someone else pay the court costs. Gamaliel Bailey, who had published the controversial antislavery novel *Uncle Tom's Cabin* and was editor of the antislavery newspaper *National Era*, promised to raise the money for court costs and other expenses.

Forty-one-year-old Montgomery Blair, a citizen of Missouri, was an able and skilled lawyer. He had practiced law in St. Louis for a number of years before moving to Washington in 1853. Blair had begun to practice before the high court soon after his arrival. He resembled Abraham Lincoln (and would later become Lincoln's postmaster general) in that he was tall and awkward with a high-pitched voice and a hatred of long speeches. Blair was not an abolitionist, and he had once owned slaves, but he was dedicated to stopping the spread of slavery into free territories.

For all his credentials, Blair knew he had a fight on his hands. Sanford had now hired two of the best legal counsels to defend him, an indication that someone at last recognized the political importance of this case. The attorneys were Henry S. Geyer, who had defeated the longtime Missouri Senator Thomas Hart Benton and was well known in Missouri courts, and Reverdy Johnson, a former senator from Maryland and attorney general under President Zachary Taylor. Johnson was without peer in the field of constitutional law.

Blair tried but failed to get other legal assistance. He believed that prominent lawyers were unwilling to get involved in what was beginning to look to some like an explosive case during an election year (1856). Blair would go it alone.

The case of *Dred Scott* v. *John F. A. Sandford* was officially filed with the U.S. Supreme Court on December 30, 1854. To no one's surprise, it was put off until the following term. The reason for the delay was the crowded schedule. Dred Scott would have to wait until February 1856 for yet another day in court to decide if he was a free man.

# THree

# A CASE FOR JUDICIAL RESTRAINT

THE year was 1856; the setting was the nation's
capital, Washington, D.C. The mood of the country was
edgy. The Kansas-Nebraska Act had become law and the
reactions to it were increasingly hostile. Kansas itself was
in near open revolt. Out of this turmoil, a new political
force, the Republican Party, was forming. Its members
generally placed the national interest above states' rights
and opposed slavery. President Franklin Pierce, a
Democrat, was in the White House. Although Pierce
wanted to run again for the presidency, he need not
have worried about the Republicans. His views on slavery (he thought of abolitionists as fanatics) and the
mess in Kansas would do him in. The Democrats nominated and won with James Buchanan instead. The
newly formed Republicans would not be a force until
1860, with the election of Abraham Lincoln.

Congress was bogged down in trying to elect a
Speaker of the House and in angry debate over what
should be done about Kansas. Newspapers carried every
argument back and forth, but they still were not printing much about Dred Scott, and so the public remained
largely unaware of the case.

## THe Taney court

In 1856, nine justices sat on the Supreme Court of the United States when the case of *Scott* v. *Sandford* came before it. The number of Supreme Court justices has not been fixed through the years. With the Judiciary Act of 1789, the Supreme Court originally had five justices, with a sixth added in 1790 and a seventh in 1807. The number was increased to nine in 1837 and would briefly jump to ten during the Civil War. Adding the tenth judge was a political move that gave the Court a pro-Union majority. The number was reduced to seven in 1867 and increased again to nine in 1869, where it remains.

The Taney Court of eight associate justices and one chief justice was geographically balanced. Five justices were from slave states and belonged to slaveholding families, although two did not hold slaves. The other four had always lived in free states. Seven were Democrats, one was a Republican, and one a Whig. The Whig Party was organized in the United States in 1834 and was active for about twenty years. As a conservative group, the Whigs' main political purpose was to rally against what they regarded as the tyranny of President Andrew Jackson. When their last presidential candidate, General Winfield Scott, failed miserably in 1854, most of the Whigs flocked to either the Democrats or Republicans.

Longest on the Court at the time of *Dred Scott* was an Ohio Republican, John McLean, born in New Jersey in 1785. He was appointed by Andrew Jackson, and his term of office was from 1829 to 1861. McLean had been a member of the Ohio Supreme Court, a congressman, and a U.S. postmaster general. Although never nominated, McLean "made himself available" in all presidential

# THE U.S. COURT SYSTEM

The Judiciary Act of 1789 established the court system of the United States; the Constitution had set out only the barest of outlines for the third branch of government after the executive and legislative. The act was the result of a long, testy struggle, and most members thought it was only a temporary compromise. However, many historians agree that the act was one of the most important legislative pieces ever enacted by the Congress.

The Judiciary Act provided for a three-tiered judicial system, set up like a pyramid. At the top is the Supreme Court of the United States, the highest level in the U.S. legal system. The middle tier contained three circuit courts covering the eastern, middle, and southern United States. At first, two judges from the Supreme Court had to preside over the circuit courts twice a year. At that time the only court of appeals was the Supreme Court. Today, the circuit courts are called courts of appeal and have their own judges. The bottom layer of the legal pyramid contains the district courts, which hear most of the everyday cases. There were originally thirteen district courts set up in main cities, with one judge each.

campaigns between 1832 and 1860. McLean's love was politics, and his ambitions always remained more political than judicial. However, he did believe that a free black was a U.S. citizen. McLean was known for nonpartisan and antislavery attitudes.

James M. Wayne joined the high court in 1835, leaving his position as state judge in Georgia. He stayed on the bench until 1867. A Democrat born in Savannah in 1790, he had also been the city's mayor, a state legislator, and a three-term congressman. Andrew Jackson, whom Wayne strongly supported, appointed him. A southerner, Wayne remained loyal to the Union during the Civil War. He, along with Taney, were the two non-slaveholding southerners on the bench.

A Democrat from Nashville, Tennessee, John Catron, born in Virginia in 1786, served on the Court from 1837 until his death in 1865. He was a member of Tennessee's Supreme Court of Last Resort, where, in his most famous decision, he disbarred a lawyer for dueling. Catron was for states' rights. Also appointed by Jackson, whom he strongly supported, he generally cast his vote with the chief justice.

Peter V. Daniel served on the Supreme Court from 1841 to 1860. Born in Virginia in 1784, he had been a U.S. district judge, a state legislator, and the state's lieutenant governor. A Democrat, Daniel was appointed by Martin Van Buren and was a lifelong Jeffersonian and upholder of states' rights.

Samuel Nelson (1792–1873) was a New Yorker and a Democrat. A hard-working, noncontroversial justice, he was appointed by John Tyler in 1845. Nelson retired in the fall of 1872 and died the following year.

Another northerner and Democrat, Robert C. Grier was born in Pennsylvania in 1794 and joined the Court in 1846, serving until 1870. He sat on the District Court of Allegheny County until his appointment to the high bench by James K. Polk. Grier was a staunch Unionist during the Civil War.

The lone Whig was Harvard graduate Benjamin R. Curtis (1809–1874), a state judge from Watertown, Massachusetts. Appointed by Millard Fillmore in 1851, he served on the bench just six years before resigning after a bitter public correspondence with Chief Justice Taney.

The youngest justice was John A. Campbell, a Democrat from Alabama, born in 1811. He served two terms in the Alabama legislature and was appointed to the high court in 1853 by Franklin Pierce, serving until 1861. Then, from 1862 to 1865, he was assistant secretary of war for the Confederacy.

Although seemingly well balanced in terms of geography and background, that picture of the Supreme Court is deceptive. Even though there were four northerners on the court, Nelson and Grier consistently supported slavery in all cases brought before them. Curtis was the only justice not appointed by a Democratic president (Millard Fillmore was a Whig and antislavery), and seven of the justices were appointed by southern, slaveholding presidents.

Only one justice on the Taney court, John McLean, was an open opponent of slavery. Curtis was a conservative Whig who seemed to favor the South on the issue. The other seven were Democrats (including Taney): five southerners who were clearly proslavery, plus Nelson and Grier. Daniel was fanatic in his opposition to black rights; Wayne firmly supported slavery; Campbell and Catron were more sympathetic to states' rights. Campbell would even leave the Court in 1861 to join the Confederacy.

ASSOCIATE JUSTICE BENJAMIN R. CURTIS OF MASSACHUSETTS DISSENTED FROM CHIEF JUSTICE ROGER TANEY'S DECISION IN THE *DRED SCOTT* CASE.

# Democrats, Republicans, Whigs, and Know-Nothings

During the years that the *Dred Scott* case was grinding through the legal system, the U.S. government was largely in the hands of four political parties—one was around for a while, one was just forming, one was just leaving, and one lasted a short term. The Democratic Party can be traced to 1792, to Thomas Jefferson and the Jeffersonian Republicans; it adopted its present name with Andrew Jackson in the 1830s. The Republicans, or Grand Old Party (GOP), formed in 1854, uniting former Whigs, Democrats, and Free-Soilers. The name appealed to those who generally placed national interest above states' rights.

The Whigs, whose name was borrowed from the British party of the same name, were on their way out (Curtis was the lone Whig on the Court) at the time of the *Dred Scott* trial. Active from 1834 to 1854, the party was organized mainly to fight Jackson's policies. The Whigs became a force in 1840, when they controlled both House and Senate and got William Henry Harrison elected to the White House in 1841. Harrison died within a month of his inauguration, and was succeeded by another Whig, John Tyler. Tyler vetoed most major Whig legislation. Zachary Taylor, also a Whig, was elected in 1848; he died in office in 1850. Millard Fillmore succeeded Taylor as the last of the Whigs. By 1854 most of the Whigs had joined the new Republicans, and some found a home with the short-lived Know-Nothings.

Also known as the American Party, the Know-Nothings flourished in the 1850s. The party was an outgrowth of anti-immigrant and anti-Roman Catholic sentiment that sprang up in the 1840s. The increase in immigrants was seen as a threat to native-born workers, who began to organize in secret groups. When asked about their activities, they were supposed to say that they "knew nothing" and hence the name. The party reached its peak in 1855 when Congress had five senators and forty-three representatives from the Know-Nothings. After that, the Know-Nothings became divided over the issue of slavery. Many of its members joined the recently created Republican Party. By the 1860 presidential elections, the Know-Nothings had died as a national party.

The odds did not seem to be in Dred Scott's favor. Nor did the looming figure of the fifth chief justice of the U.S. Supreme Court, Roger Taney of Maryland, who was known to be proslavery.

## THE CHIEF JUSTICE

Born in Calvert County, Maryland, on March 17, 1777, Roger Brooke Taney grew up well-to-do, on the slave-holding tobacco farm of his parents, Michael and Monica Brooke Taney. He was one of seven children. As a young man, Taney was tall and gaunt with a tendency to stoop, and had nearsighted eyes that made him squint. He had a long face, a prominent nose, and thick black hair. The fact that he was considered homely, some even said ugly, made him shy.

Roger Taney had one great asset—a brilliant mind. He also had a father who was determined to give his four sons a good start in life. Michael Taney was born in England and educated in Catholic schools in France. During his early years, his son Roger walked three miles to and from the nearest school with his elder brother and sister. That school was not stimulating enough for Roger, so he was sent to a boarding school about ten miles away. After boarding school, Taney was tutored at home by a graduate of Princeton, who urged Taney's father to send him to college. So Taney enrolled at Dickinson College in Carlisle, Pennsylvania. Founded in 1783 by Dr. Benjamin Rush, a surgeon general in the Continental Army, the school had such a good reputation that Taney's staunchly Catholic father overlooked the fact that the college was founded by a Presbyterian. In those days, such labels carried considerably more weight than they do now.

Taney returned home to Maryland in 1795 after graduating from Dickinson as class valedictorian. He had completed the four-year course in three years and was now eighteen years old. Interestingly, around that time little Dickinson College would graduate a future chief justice (Taney), a future associate justice (Grier), and a future president (James Buchanan).

After a winter of relaxing in the countryside and fox-hunting with his father, Taney decided it was time to find a career. Since the eldest son would inherit the family tobacco plantation, the other boys were expected to work at something else. Taney decided on the law. At that time, young men entered that profession by paying for the honor of reading law in a lawyer's or judge's office for about three years. The best place for studying law was Annapolis, Maryland, which was the seat of the state general court. Annapolis was not yet the home of the U.S. Naval Academy, founded in 1845.

Taney studied law with Judge Jeremiah Townley Chase, a former member of the Continental Congress. He was also a delegate of the convention that ratified the U.S. Constitution, which he opposed. Chase was viewed as a judge of exceptional qualities. After staying with Chase for three years, Taney left and was admitted to the bar in Annapolis on June 17, 1799. Two days later he tried his first case, which he won, although the defendant was too poor to pay a fee. Next, Taney served one year in the Maryland House of Delegates before he settled down in Frederick, Maryland, to practice law.

During that period, Taney became friends with Francis Scott Key, who wrote the "Star-Spangled Banner," and with Key's sister, Anne, whom he would marry in 1806. Right from the start, the marriage was one of devotion but also diplomacy. Roger Taney, a Catholic, and Anne Key, an Episcopalian, agreed they would raise any sons as Catholics and any daughters as Episcopalians. The Taneys eventually had six surviving children, all of whom were reared Episcopalians.

Taney returned to the Maryland House of Delegates in 1816, where he was often involved in matters of finance and banking, and was elected to the state senate. His term expired in 1821, and two years later, he moved with his family to Baltimore and was soon recognized as an excellent attorney. Juries noted not only his sense of fair play but also his fairness in dealing with opposing counsel. In 1827, he was appointed attorney general of Maryland. By now a staunch backer of Andrew Jackson, Taney became attorney general of the United States when the president reorganized his cabinet in 1831.

A fight over the Bank of the United States put Taney into the national spotlight. He led the Democrats' opposition to a central bank, which they thought of as being mainly a tool of eastern financial interests. Congress had chartered the second Bank of the United States in 1816, but the charter was due to expire unless renewed in 1836. Although privately owned and operated and generally free from public regulation, the bank was the official depository of U.S. government funds, and five of its twenty-five directors were appointed by the president with the Senate's "advise and consent."

President Jackson believed that the bank held too much power and was against renewing the charter. This position put him in opposition to the bank president, Nicholas Biddle, who applied early for a new charter, which was easily passed by Congress in 1832. The bank became a main issue in the presidential election that

A POLITICAL CARTOON SHOWS PRESIDENT ANDREW JACKSON IN 1832 BRAN-
DISHING AN "ORDER FOR THE REMOVAL OF THE PUBLIC MONEY DEPOSITED
IN THE UNITED STATES BANK." CHIEF JUSTICE ROGER TANEY SIDED WITH
THE PRESIDENT.

year between Jackson and Henry Clay. Jackson won and
felt that his victory gave him a mandate to destroy the
bank. He ordered that no more government funds be
deposited there. Taney sided with the president, urging
him to veto the bill that renewed the bank's charter, as
Jackson did. Taney also wrote much of the veto message
explaining the president's opposition.

# THe secOND BaNK OF THe UNITeD STaTes

One of the most important decisions of the Supreme Court led by Chief Justice John Marshall was *McCulloch* v. *Maryland* (1819). This case spelled out what was meant by the "necessary and proper" clause in the U.S. Constitution. It involved the right of Congress to authorize the Second Bank of the United States, as well as a state's right to tax a federal government institution. The First Bank of the United States was the idea of Secretary of the Treasury Alexander Hamilton in 1791; its charter expired in 1811. After the Second Bank was chartered in 1816, several states that were against the national bank passed laws to tax its branches. When James McCulloch, cashier of the Baltimore branch, refused to pay the tax, the dispute wound up in the Supreme Court.

The Court said that the Maryland tax was unconstitutional. Marshall used a loose interpretation of the Constitution to affirm the power of Congress to create the bank in the first place. He said that although the Constitution does not specifically give Congress such power, it does not rule it out. The Court also decided that a state's power to tax is subordinate to the Constitution. That victory for the bank ended with Jackson's veto of its charter in 1832. However, in the twentieth century, Franklin Roosevelt's New Deal and other such legislation was based on this decision as a starting point for government involvement in social and other programs.

Jackson appointed Taney secretary of the treasury in 1833. However, for the first time, the Congress refused to confirm a president's nominee to a cabinet post. Taney had made strong enemies with his opposition to the bank charter.

After the president's action, Biddle in turn called in bank loans, a move that led to a financial crisis. Clay pushed a resolution through Congress in 1834 censuring Jackson, but the president held firm. When the bank charter finally expired, Biddle got a state charter from Pennsylvania to operate the bank. It went out of business in 1841.

## on the high court

In 1835 Jackson nominated Taney to be an associate justice of the U.S. Supreme Court. The nomination seemed somewhat badly timed since Congress had so recently rejected Taney as a cabinet member, but to wait for a new Senate to vote would mean delaying an entire year. Taney's enemies were still strong, and they stalled the nomination. Then, on July 6, about two months before his eightieth birthday, Chief Justice John Marshall died in Philadelphia.

There was much speculation about his successor. Most thought it would be Justice Joseph Story, a staunch Federalist who believed in a strong federal government and who had been on the court since 1811. In December, Jackson submitted Taney's name. Both Jackson and Taney were advocates of states' rights. The Senate at the time consisted of forty-eight members, half for Jackson and half against. Taney was confirmed in March by a vote of 29 to 15, and he took the oath of office on April 8, at the age of fifty-nine.

Roger Brooke Taney became chief justice over the opposition of many powerful politicians. Despite the many decisions rendered during his tenure, he would be forever associated with the *Dred Scott* case.

When Taney was appointed to the highest seat in the legal system, he had a very tough act to follow. Historians frequently call Marshall the nation's greatest chief justice. In *Marbury* v. *Madison* (1803), Marshall established the power of judicial review for the Court. This gave the Court the right to declare both federal and state laws unconstitutional when they were brought before the Court as the result of a suit. Actually, the two men had a good deal in common. They were both totally devoted to the Court, strong in their reliance on the Constitution, and excellent writers. They were also devoted to their wives and families but ill at ease in large gatherings. Both were tall, shy, and dressed rather sloppily, although Taney was less formal than Marshall in his attire on the bench. Marshall always wore the traditional knee breeches (a custom of the English courts), while Taney favored long trousers. Even beyond looks, however, there was no mistaking a Marshall Court for a Taney Court. Under Marshall the Supreme Court had risen to a position of power, although in Marshall's last years, the dynamic power of the Jackson era forced the high Court to speak with less authority. Most noticeable was the Court's more lenient attitude toward the power of state legislatures. The Taney Court tended to use power sparingly when it came to dealing with issues that concerned disagreements between the U.S. Constitution and state governments.

When Taney became chief justice, many thought he would not have a very long tenure on the bench, as he was constantly fussing about some real or imagined ailment. Although he did suffer from rheumatism and later in life was very frail, he remained on the Court for twenty-eight years. A soft-spoken man of simple tastes, he presided over the Court in a gentle but firm manner. His opinions were written simply and to the point.

On Monday, January 9, 1837, the day Taney first sat on the bench, the Court did not have the look of a place of great power and importance. At the time the courtroom was the old Senate chamber. (The Supreme Court did not get its own building until 1935.) The *New York Tribune* called it "a potato hole of a place . . . a queer room of small dimensions and shaped overhead like a quarter section of a pumpkin shell." It was heated by fireplaces and tended to be dark.

The outside of the courtroom did not look much better. Washington, D.C., was largely swampland. Since large tracts of trees had been chopped down for buildings, everything got muddy when it rained. Pennsylvania Avenue had been paved, but all the other streets were either mud holes or dustbins, depending on the weather. Mark Twain wrote that Washington was a "City of Magnificent Intentions, with broad avenues that begin in nothing and lead nowhere."

The Supreme Court of 1837 met promptly at eleven every morning except Sunday. The justices worked until three, when all other government offices closed. The usual dinner hour was at four o'clock.

Roger Brooke Taney became chief justice despite the strong opposition of powerful politicians such as Henry Clay, Daniel Webster, and John C. Calhoun. Nevertheless, in time many of his enemies came to respect Taney, who believed, as did Marshall, in the sovereignty of the federal court. Taney did, however, also profess the conservative tradition associated with southern aristocracy. His views on what the courts could do about slavery never changed. He had inherited slaves, but he freed them in 1818 and 1821 and on one occasion even helped a slave to buy his freedom. Despite those actions, Taney opposed any federal limitations on slavery itself, believing that power rested with the states.

Not long after becoming chief justice, Taney made his mark in *Charles River Bridge Company* v. *Warren Bridge Company* (1837). The case concerned the rights of private property versus those of society. In 1785 Massachusetts authorized the Charles River Bridge Company to build a bridge from Charlestown to Boston and collect tolls. In 1828 the legislature allowed the businessmen of Charlestown to build a new Warren Bridge. The merchants were authorized to collect tolls on the new bridge until they recouped their money; then the bridge would be free. The Charles River builders did not want to lose their monopoly, so they sued to stop construction on the grounds that the new bridge violated their contract with the state.

Taney upheld the right of the state to contract with another company to build a competing bridge. In siding against Charles River and for the public interest, Taney said, "While the rights of private property are sacredly guarded, we must not forget that the community also have rights, and that the happiness and well-being of every citizen depends on their faithful preservation."

## A case for judicial restraint

Judicial restraint is a general term that says the court should confine its use of power according to the principles of separation of powers. The function of the court should be separate from that of the legislature. The court should not take on a dispute if its decision is not going to relieve a definite injury, or if, in fact, the conflict is already over.

At the onset, it appeared that the Taney court would employ judicial restraint in the case of *Scott* v. *Sandford*. Using *Strader* v. *Graham* as a precedent, it seemed likely that the Court would confirm the Missouri high court as having the last word on its own state law. Thus, there would be no need for the Supreme Court to explore the merits of the case separately, and the Court would avoid any controversy over the issue of slavery. In February 1857, Justice Nelson began a draft that steered clear of all the problem aspects of the case. In the draft Nelson said Scott was still a slave because Missouri law said he was. That was it. Although it would have been a disappointment to the Scott forces, that decision would have settled the case without controversy.

This was apparently not the time for judicial restraint, however. The justices rejected Nelson's approach. It was unlikely, given its character, that the Taney Court would have gone along with Dred Scott's appeal. What emerged instead was an extreme proslavery position. Taney thought that he could resolve the slavery controversy by judicial decree, but instead he only increased the tension and opened himself to the charge of failed judicial leadership. Justice Wayne said that a new opinion should deal with the issues that had been sidestepped until then. Taney agreed. The Court, under the pressure of the times, seemed resolved to do what laws and politics had so far been unable to do. The Supreme Court would take on the question of slavery. In so doing, the case became a central issue in the presidential election of 1860. It is called by legal and constitutional scholars the worst decision ever rendered by the highest court in the land.

# four
# THE "WORST" DECISION

THE SUPREME COURT MET on Monday, February 11, 1856, to hear opening arguments in the case of *Scott* v. *Sandford*. Although the public was still largely unaware of the case and there was no advance publicity in the press, a few newspapers were showing signs of interest. The Washington *Evening Star* and the *National Era* noted that the trial was about to begin. The Washington-based reporter for the New York *Tribune*, James E. Harvey, offered his ideas in print about a Court decision.

## THE OPENING

Before the Court session opened, Scott's attorney, Montgomery Blair, had filed a written brief. There is no evidence that Sanford's lawyers did the same. One of the reasons might be that Sanford was by now suffering from mental illness (he would be confined to an institution by the end of the year) and was actually the defendant in name only. The real defendant had become the slaveholders of the South.

Blair declared that the Missouri court's decision had been influenced by current political conditions. It was common law, Blair said, to consider a slave to be free once he or she had lived in a free state. Basically,

Blair presented three arguments: (1) Although Scott had been a slave in Missouri, a slave state, he became free when he traveled to the free state of Illinois; (2) following the principle of "once free, always free," Scott remained a free man even when he returned to Missouri; and (3) since Scott lived in one of the states of the United States, he was therefore a citizen of that state and had a right to sue.

Although Sanford's lawyers did not submit a written file, they injected a new argument. The attorneys declared that the Missouri Compromise, which prohibited slavery in the new territories, was invalid because it was unconstitutional and, therefore, Congress did not have the right to decide on the slavery issue. If the Missouri Compromise was invalid, then the fact that Scott traveled to Illinois did not make him free. If he was not free in the first place, he remained a slave when he returned to Missouri and therefore had no standing to sue. Suddenly the question before the Court was not just Scott's freedom but whether a law passed by the U.S. Congress was unconstitutional. The real question was whether the Supreme Court would take up the challenge. Some thought the Court might just evade the slavery controversy by refusing to hear the case.

The opening arguments by both counsels took about twelve hours spread over four days. Blair now had some assistance in his corner. George T. Curtis, brother of Associate Justice Curtis, offered some limited help. Curtis, however, was known to have enforced the Fugitive Slave Act in Massachusetts, so he seemed more proslavery than Blair. Historians find it something of a puzzlement that zealots on the antislavery side never appeared to jump into the case. The fact that the case received little publicity at first and there was general turmoil in the country may have been contributing factors.

On February 22 the Court convened for discussion. When nothing was decided by May, Taney ordered the case held over until the new term, that is to say, another seven months. Then, in early January 1857, Justice Daniel's wife died in a fire at the family home, and he suffered burns while trying to rescue her. Waiting for his recovery delayed deliberations until February 14. The final decision would not be made until March 6, more than a year after it was filed and ten years after Dred and Harriet Scott had first petitioned to sue.

Each day that the decision was delayed, the country was plunging further into violence. Kansas had descended into an orgy of burning and killing. Furthermore, the mayhem was not confined to the general public. Massachusetts Senator Charles Sumner, an outspoken crusader against slavery, delivered a stinging speech in May 1856 denouncing the authors of the Kansas-Nebraska Act (Senators Stephen A. Douglas and Andrew P. Butler) as slavery advocates. Two days later in the Senate chamber, Butler's nephew, Congressman Preston S. Brooks of South Carolina, walked up to Sumner at his desk and beat him severely with a cane. It took Sumner three years to recover.

In the midst of this chaos, the Republicans and Democrats put up their candidates for the presidential election of 1856. The Republican ticket carried John C. Frémont and William L. Dayton on a strong anti-slavery program. It stated that it was the right and the duty of Congress to prohibit slavery in the territories. James Buchanan and John C. Breckinridge headed the Democratic slate, running on a policy of popular

SOUTHERN CHIVALRY — ARGUMENT VERSUS CLUB'S.

VIOLENCE OVER SLAVERY SPILLED OVER ONTO THE SENATE FLOOR. SENATOR CHARLES SUMNER WAS BEATEN SO BADLY BY A FELLOW CONGRESSMAN OVER A SPEECH HE GAVE AGAINST SLAVERY THAT HE DIDN'T RECOVER FOR THREE YEARS.

REPUBLICAN JOHN C. FRÉMONT RAN ON AN ANTISLAVERY SLATE IN THE PRESIDENTIAL
ELECTION OF 1856. HE WAS DEFEATED.

sovereignty—letting the residents of the territories decide for themselves. The Democrats squeaked in on November 4. Such was the atmosphere in the United States as the Taney Court discussed the future of Dred Scott.

On December 15, 1856, the U.S. Supreme Court met to hear rearguments in the case. The national election was over, and tempers seemed calm for the moment. The atmosphere was not helped, however, by President Pierce's last annual State of the Union message. Humiliated at being denied the nomination by his own party, he nonetheless called the Democratic victory a personal triumph for the proslavery side. At least by now, with news of the case carried in a good deal of the press, most of the reading public had heard the name Dred Scott.

Blair and Curtis spent the first day of arguments declaring that Scott was a citizen and therefore could sue. They also stressed that Congress had the right to make decisions about slavery in the territories and that the states had the right to prohibit slavery.

When it was the defense's turn, Geyer and Johnson argued, as they had earlier, that since Scott was a Negro, he was not a U.S. citizen and so could not sue.

Further, they claimed that living in Illinois temporarily did not make Scott free. Finally, they claimed the Missouri Compromise was unconstitutional on two grounds. First, the compromise's banning of slavery in the territories was against the interests of slave states. Since Congress could not pass laws that were against the interests of the states, the compromise was unconstitutional. Second, the compromise violated the authority of the people because it took away their power over local government, which the Constitution guaranteed. So, again, the Missouri Compromise was unconstitutional.

## THe court Deliberates

The Court was now faced with four decisions, the first being whether there was a plea in abatement before the Court. A "plea in abatement" is a request to throw out a case because it has no merit. In that event, the Court would simply refuse to rule at all. In the *Dred Scott* case, there was the question of whether Scott was a citizen of Missouri, a status that would give him the right to sue, and also the question of whether Scott was free because he had lived in the free state of Illinois. In addition, there was the question of Congress having the power to prohibit slavery in the territories. In other words, was the Missouri Compromise legal?

## THe CHOICes

The Supreme Court did not have to take up the challenge presented by Sanford's lawyers concerning the constitutionality of the Missouri Compromise. Instead the Court could decide Scott's freedom in one of two simpler ways. The Court could rule that, yes, there was a plea to throw out the case because it had no merit, and no, Scott was not a citizen of Missouri—because he was black—and therefore could not sue. A Court decision to dismiss the case because it had no jurisdiction might have angered some abolitionists, but most northerners would not have argued. They might be against slavery, but not many would have fought over black citizenship.

An even simpler solution would have been for the Court to agree with the decision of the lower Missouri court: Scott's residence in free territory did not make him a free man. In the end, the Supreme Court did not choose a simple solution.

The charged atmosphere that awaited the Supreme Court's decision was not soothed by the incoming president, James Buchanan. Delivering his inaugural address just two days before Taney offered the Court's ruling, Buchanan noted that there was a "difference of opinion" about slavery and who should decide its status in the territories. Said the new president,

> This is, happily, a matter of but little practical importance. Besides, it is a judicial question, which legitimately belongs to the Supreme Court of the United States, before whom it is now pending, and will, it is understood, be speedily and finally settled. To their decision, in common with all good citizens, I shall cheerfully submit, whatever this may be.

The president's remarks were somewhat less than honest. In fact, he had already been told of the decision. Justice Robert C. Grier, like Buchanan a Pennsylvanian, had kept the then-president elect informed of the proceedings. Buchanan was trying to help the nation to accept the decision that he, along with Taney, really wanted. As for his prediction about the judicial question, it was anything but "speedily and finally settled."

## THE DECISION
On Friday, March 6, 1857, Chief Justice Roger Taney read the decision of the U.S. Supreme Court in the case of *Scott* v. *Sandford*. The courtroom was crowded. As Walter Lewis described the scene in his biography of Taney:

> Illness, coupled with the fatigue and exposure of the [presidential] Inauguration ceremonies had exhausted the Chief Justice, who eleven days later would be eighty. During the two hours it took him to read his opinion his voice occasionally

dropped to a whisper. This not only gave his words an impression of weakness but led to faulty reporting in the newspapers, and the defects were not rectified until the decision was officially published on May 29. Justices McLean and Curtis [who dissented], on the other hand, gave copies of their opinions to the press and they were widely distributed long before the Court Reporter released official copies of the opinions.

The decision read by Taney was reported as the majority opinion of the Court. However, only Wayne agreed with Taney on all points. Weakened or not, the decision of the Supreme Court, by a vote of seven to two, kept Dred Scott in the status of a slave. It had taken eleven years to come full circle.

Here is what the Court decided:

On the question of abatement, four of the justices (Taney, Wayne, Daniel, and Curtis) ruled that the case was properly before the Court.

On the question of citizenship, three of the justices (Taney, Wayne, and Daniel) said that a black man could not be a U.S. citizen, and if Scott was not a citizen of Missouri, then he had no right to sue in a federal court. Therefore, the lower court had been in error when it ruled on his citizenship and never had the jurisdiction to rule in the first place. The judges said blacks could not be citizens because they were not—and were not meant to be—included in the definition of a citizen in the Constitution.

Seven justices (Taney, Wayne, Grier, Daniel, Campbell, Nelson, and Catron) said that Missouri laws determined Scott's status after he returned from Illinois; therefore, he was still a slave. Residence in Illinois did not make him free, said the Court, because his status depended on the laws in Missouri.

THE POLITICAL QUADRILLE IS A PARODY OF HOW THE *DRED SCOTT* CASE AFFECTED PRESIDENTIAL POLITICS. DRED SCOTT, SEATED IN THE MIDDLE, PLAYS THE FIDDLE WHILE DEMOCRATIC AND REPUBLICAN POLITICIANS DANCE TO HIS TUNE.

# DISSenTInG OPInIOns

The Supreme Court of the United States decided on March 6, 1857, that Dred Scott was still a slave by a vote of 7 to 2. The two dissenting opinions were voiced by John McLean and Benjamin Curtis. McLean's opinion was published in May after the decision, but it had appeared in the *New York Tribune* earlier in March. Some say he deliberately gave out an advance copy so his views would be spread quickly and accurately. He was especially forceful and defiant in denouncing the majority opinion that slaves were property.

The lengthy dissenting opinion of Justice Curtis (at seventy pages, it was sixteen pages longer than Taney's majority opinion) has been quoted more often than the majority opinion and became a political document during the elections of 1858 and 1860. On the subject of whether Congress had the power to prohibit slavery in the territories, Curtis was adamant. Nothing in the Constitution prevented Congress from prohibiting slavery in the territories or protecting it for that matter, and the Constitution was the only proof he could accept. Since there was no such proof, no one could object to an act of Congress (such as the Missouri Compromise) that prohibited slavery in the territories. So, declared Curtis, Scott should be a free man. Curtis declared that birth was always tied to citizenship in Anglo-American law and that by allowing slavery in the territories, all of the laws of a slave society are also allowed into the territories. He wrote,

> the rights, powers, and obligations, which grow out of that status [of a slave], must be defined, protected, and enforced, by such laws. The liability of the master for the torts and crimes of his

slave, and of third persons for assaulting or injuring or harboring or kidnapping him, the forms and modes of emancipation and sale, their subjection to the debts of the master, succession by death of the master, suits for freedom, the capacity of the slave to be party to a suit, or to be a witness, with such police regulations as have existed in all civilized States where slavery has been tolerated, are among the subjects upon which municipal legislation becomes neccssary when slavery is introduced.

# WHat makes a citizen?

Much of the argument in the *Dred Scott* case, from the lower courts to the Supreme Court, concerned Scott's status as a citizen of Missouri. Was he indeed a citizen? The framers of the U.S. Constitution provided no definition of citizenship. Article I of the Constitution refers to citizenship—saying that members of Congress must be citizens—but does not define the term. The Constitution says the president must be a "natural-born citizen," a phrase that implies that citizenship results from birth within a territory. The Taney Court's decision that someone of African descent could not be a citizen was erased by the Fourteenth Amendment, passed in 1868, which said that anyone born or naturalized in the United States was a citizen. However, even the Fourteenth Amendment did not settle the matter entirely. In 1884 the Court ruled in *Elk* v. *Wilkins* that Native Americans were not automatically citizens, saying that, as members of tribes, they were not wholly under the jurisdiction of the federal government. However, that ruling was later reversed by Congress.

Through the years, the Supreme Court has heard many cases that involve interpretation of the citizen's right to vote. This right cannot be denied on account of race (Fifteenth Amendment) or failure to pay a poll tax or other tax (Twenty-fourth), or age (Twenty-sixth), but in no case has the concept of citizenship itself been at the core of the problem. So the Court seems to reflect the Constitution's own vagueness on just what citizenship is.

Six justices (Taney, Wayne, Grier, Daniel, Campbell, and Catron) declared that the Missouri Compromise was invalid. Scott's claim to be a free man because of his residence at Fort Snelling was invalid because the Missouri Compromise, said the Court, was unconstitutional from the start. It was unconstitutional because it violated the Fifth Amendment, which states that Congress can pass no law that deprives someone of "life, liberty, or property, without due process of law." (Taney grouped humans along with things under the heading of "property.") In other words, the Court said that, by giving Scott his freedom, the Missouri Compromise was taking away Sanford's property— Scott—without due process. For the first time since 1803, in the *Marbury v. Madison* case, the Supreme Court had decided a law to be unconstitutional.

In his study of the case, Paul Finkelman concluded that Taney's proslavery opinions did not grow from the turmoil of the times but were his lifelong views that were put to the test here: "Taney's support of states' rights on issues of race and the rights of free blacks [when he was attorney general] anticipated the views he later articulated in *Dred Scott*."

As attorney general, Taney had to comment on the constitutional power of southern states to prohibit free blacks (from other states or the British Empire) from entering their jurisdiction.

In his official *Opinion of the Attorney General*, Taney asserted:

> The African race in the United States even when free, are everywhere a degraded class, and exercise no political influence. The privileges they are allowed to enjoy, are accorded to them as a matter

of kindness and benevolence rather than right. . . .
They are not looked upon as citizens by the con-
tracting parties who formed the Constitution. They
were evidently not supposed to be included in the
term *citizens*.

In his opinion, Taney also asserted that the
Declaration of Independence was never meant to apply
to blacks, who were, in the attorney general's mind, not
entitled to the natural rights of "life, liberty, and the
pursuit of happiness."

This official opinion of the attorney general
demonstrates that the antiblack, proslavery views Taney
expressed in *Dred Scott* were not an aberration or a
function of the changing politics of the 1850s. Rather,
these views were part of his lifelong ideology.

These themes were also part of Taney's majority opinion on *Dred Scott*. He argued against citizenship for blacks
entirely on the basis of race. Although his statement was
not accurate, he said that all blacks had been slaves when
the nation was founded, or that even those who were free
had never had any legal or political rights. According to
Taney, blacks could not claim

the rights and privileges which that instrument [the
Constitution] provides for and secures to citizens of the
United States. On the contrary, they were at that time
[1787] considered as a subordinate and inferior class of
beings, who had been subjugated by the dominant
race, and, whether emancipated or not, yet remained
subject to their authority, and had no rights or privileges but such as those who held the power and the
Government might choose to grant them.

The decision of the Supreme Court, if accepted by the American people, would also have a desirable political effect. At least that was the hope of Taney, Buchanan, and others who feared the growing presence of the Republican Party. The Republicans had lost the election of 1856; nevertheless, the party's showing was impressive, and it gave no signs of disappearing. Yet if the party's main platform was based on stopping the spread of slavery in the territories and if Congress had no power to forbid slavery, then the Republicans would have no reason to exist.

## THE OPPOSITION

Both John McLean and Benjamin Curtis gave lengthy statements declaring their reasons for disagreeing with the Court's ruling. Curtis argued that the Constitution did not take away citizenship from anyone who already had it and that blacks held citizenship under the Articles of Confederation, which preceded the Constitution. He also argued that the Court had no right to rule on the validity of the Missouri Compromise.

Before and after the decision, Curtis and Taney engaged in increasingly bitter correspondence stemming from the early release of Curtis's dissenting opinion. When Curtis asked for a copy of Taney's opinion before it was delivered, he was turned down. Taney implied that Curtis wanted the copy to use as propaganda against the majority decision. Wrote Taney,

> It would seem from your letter to me that you sup-
> pose you are entitled to demand it as a right,
> being one of the members of the tribunal. This
> would undoubtedly be the case if you wished it to

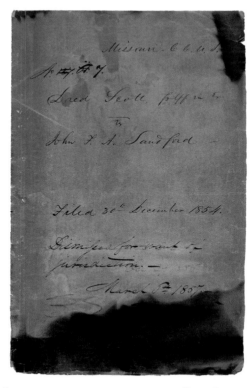

THE *DRED SCOTT* DECISION, AS HANDED DOWN BY CHIEF JUSTICE ROGER TANEY.

aid you in the discharge of your official duties. But I understood you as not desiring or intending it for that purpose. On the contrary, you announced from the Bench that you regarded this opinion as extrajudicial—and not binding upon you or anyone else.

Curtis was stung by the sharpness of the reply. Even though the Court's decision in May made the whole argument moot, Curtis was uncomfortable enough to resign from the Court in September. According to the historian Don Fehrenbacher, Taney's personal animosity to Curtis is evident here: "Curtis . . . was one of the Court's newest and youngest members—in Taney's eyes, a veritable whippersnapper and a typical product of New England hypocrisy."

## justice finally delivered

There are no reports of who told Dred Scott about the Court's decision or how he reacted. The decision changed his life very little at first. It is somewhat ironic, though, that the Court's decision to keep Scott a slave would open the door to his freedom.

Eleven years had passed since the first suit was filed. Scott was now working as a janitor in the law offices of Roswell Field. Days after the decision, the controversy surrounding Scott got more complicated when a Massachusetts newspaper said that Sanford was not Scott's owner after all, and that he belonged to Calvin Chaffee, Irene Emerson's new husband. Chaffee claimed his wife had told him only months before that the Supreme Court case involved the man who was her slave. The decision had little effect on

# THe MecHanics OF FreeDom

Obtaining one's freedom in a slave state could be quite complicated, as proven by the case of Dred Scott. Even when the slave's owner was willing, there were certain procedures to follow. Under Missouri law, a slave could be emancipated only by an owner who was a citizen of that state. Therefore, Irene Emerson Chaffee or her husband could not have given Scott his freedom if they had wanted to. So Chaffee first had to execute a so-called quitclaim, which gave up any rights or interests that he, his wife, and his daughter had in Scott and his family. Those rights were transferred to Taylor Blow back in St. Louis. Blow and the Scotts appeared in the Circuit Court of St. Louis. Arba N. Crane, a lawyer who had worked in the office of Roswell Field, drew up the papers, and Judge Alexander Hamilton gave the Scott family its freedom.

Sanford himself; mentally ill for some time, he died in an institution on May 5.

Chaffee signed away any rights concerning Dred Scott. All rights were transferred to Taylor Blow, a longtime friend and ally of the Scotts. On May 26, 1857, Dred and Harriet Scott appeared in court before Judge Alexander Hamilton, who had judged his case ten years earlier. Taylor Blow signed the papers, and Dred and Harriet Scott and their two daughters were finally free.

Scott and his wife apparently lived quietly in St. Louis, although no accounts survive of how Scott earned a living. However he spent his time, Scott had less than two years of freedom to enjoy. According to Walter Ehrlich in his study of Scott, "Apparently he worked also as a porter in some of the hotels, at least one of which was the locally famous Barnum's Hotel, on Second and Walnut streets. There he did all sorts of odd jobs, but he was especially just there, an attraction for hotel guests, who could claim later that they had once seen and talked to the famous Dred Scott."

After a few weeks of illness, Scott died—probably of tuberculosis—on September 17, 1858. He was buried in an unmarked grave in Wesleyan Cemetery but was reburied by Taylor Blow, in 1867, at the family plot at Calvary Cemetery in St. Louis. This quiet little man who had merely wanted his freedom was at the time of his death the nation's most famous former slave. The back of his gravestone reads, "Dred Scott Subject of the Decision of the Supreme Court of the United States in 1857 Which Denied Citizenship to the Negro, Voided the Missouri Compromise Act, Became One of the Events That Resulted in the Civil War."

After eleven long years, the *Dred Scott* case was

DRED SCOTT

finally over, but the aftermath was just beginning. The decisions handed down by the Taney Court would go far beyond the question of freedom for one black slave. The ruling gave southerners an advantage in the slavery question now that the nation's highest court had said it was legal. It also gave the South confidence on the issue and perhaps made it more inflexible. The Supreme Court ruling contributed to the Civil War in that it deepened the long-existing wounds over the question of slavery in a divided nation.

# FIVE
# THE LONG PATH TO JUSTICE

NOT SURPRISINGLY, THere WAS great joy in the South when Taney read the Court's extreme proslavery position in the case of Dred Scott. The Richmond, Virginia, *Enquirer* called the Court "a tribunal of jurists, as learned, impartial and unprejudiced as perhaps the world has ever seen." Meanwhile, the North smouldered with anger. Said the New York *Tribune*, "Our liberties may be subverted, our rights trampled upon; the spirit of our institutions utterly disregarded."

The *Dred Scott* case did not start the trouble over slavery, but it certainly made the trouble worse. It unleashed a violent reaction from people on both sides. From the press and the pulpit and from the halls of Congress came scathing denunciations of the decision as well as an equally vigorous defense of it. The St. Louis *Evening News* proclaimed, "The recent Dred Scott decision of the Supreme Court has roused the lately torpid Northern pulpit into a factitious frenzy on the stale Negro question, and incited the preachers to a fresh crusade against the Judges." Henry Ward Beecher's paper, *The Independent*, regarded Taney's decision as "a concatenation of corrupt opinions and falsehoods" and added that it "out-Herods Herod himself."

# THe HeaDLInes

After the *Dred Scott* decision, newspapers from the North and South reflected the conflicting views of the nation.

Albany (NY) *Evening Journal*: "Judge Taney requests the American people to believe that the framers of the Constitution did not know their own minds."

The paper also said of the Court, "Five of its nine silk gowns are worn by Slaveholders."

Charleston (SC) *Mercury*: "Slavery is guaranteed by the constitutional compact."

New York *Tribune*: "Auctions of black men may be held in front of Faneuil Hall [in Boston]."

Natchez (MS) *Courier*: "This is a seeming blow at the doctrine of squatter sovereignty, but not quite as hard a one as we could wish the Court had given."

The Columbus (WI) *Republican Journal* lamented, "It strikes at the very vitals of our free institutions."

The Richmond (VA) *Enquirer* declared, " . . . if they would *let us alone* and leave slavery to the states, and to the same protection and privileges enjoyed by all other property under the Constitution, the *agitation* would come to an end on the instant."

Congress was no less spirited in its attacks and defenses. The following February, Senator Lyman Trumbull of Illinois proposed spending one thousand dollars for a bust of Taney to be placed beside those of other chief justices in the Supreme Court room. Senator Benjamin Wade of Ohio thought the money would be better spent to hang Taney in effigy. Senator William H. Seward of New York, in a speech one year after the ruling, charged that the Court's decision was based on a proslavery conspiracy between President Buchanan and the chief justice, with Dred Scott a pawn in the political game. Taney was so angry about the remark that he later told Samuel Tyler, his biographer, that had Seward been elected president in 1860, he would have refused to administer the oath of office, even though it is generally the duty of the chief justice to do so. Senator Judah P. Benjamin of Louisiana, in return, defended the Court, starting with a long review of the history of modern slavery. In his view, slavery was permissible under common law and normal in all the colonies. Most of Taney's constituents, however, while acknowledging the deficiences of the *Dred Scott* decision, applauded the chief justice for a lifetime of honest devotion to his country.

For his part, Taney remained fairly silent through the attacks. He understood that he would become the focal point of the antislavery faction. However, he placed a very high value on his own integrity. Rather than making vocal rebuttals, he spent much time writing a justification for his opinion in the case. During his last years on the bench, he faced hostility from the Republican administration and a war in which individual constitutional rights sometimes were swept aside.

# THe Lecompton constitution

The ruling in the case of *Scott* v. *Sandford* was interpreted in the eyes of many southerners as legalizing slavery everywhere in the country. In the year of that decision, proslavery leaders framed what is called the Lecompton (Kansas) Constitution for statehood. Its clauses protected slaveholders, and its bill of rights excluded free blacks. Adding to the frictions leading up to civil war, the constitution was rejected in a territorial election in January 1858. When President Buchanan recommended statehood for Kansas using its provisions, his proposal set Congress in an uproar. A compromise was reached by again offering the constitution to be judged by the territorial voters. They again rejected it, and Kansas entered the Union as a free state on January 29, 1861.

Antislavery partisans of all backgrounds feared that the next step would be for the Court to make slavery legal everywhere. Just at a time when the country needed the stabilizing influence of a solemn, respected legal system, it seemed as though the high court had weakened its own prestige, and now that the Court had become a part of this emotionally charged issue, many feared that more compromises were impossible. So the nation moved one step closer to civil war.

## Taney under attack

Because he was the chief justice and because he had delivered the majority opinion, Taney was the prime target for attack by antislavery advocates. His opinions were labeled false and prejudiced and characterized as *obiter dictum*, a Latin phrase that means opinions mentioned in passing. It indicates that the stated opinion is not necessary to the result but is merely the gratuitous opinion of the judge. In other words, critics said Taney did not have to deliver his comments on blacks in order to hand down a decision. He was also charged with deliberately setting out to denigrate the black race. Some historians say that his language, offensive as it may sound to modern ears, was cast in the idiom of the time and does not prove any intent to insult black people. Historians also point to the years of Taney's fine and dedicated service to the Court, which preserved the dignity and reforms of John Marshall before him. However, despite his twenty-eight years on the bench during most trying times and despite his work as a brilliant judge and fearless advocate of individual liberties for citizens, his record was lost in the furor of this one decision. His inflammatory opinion added so much fuel to the fire over the slavery issue that it could no longer be extinguished.

## OLD Brown OF Osawatomie

As tempers reached the boiling point following the *Dred Scott* decision, there was increasing violence about slavery in general. Shortly after the bloody eruption in Lawrence, Kansas, on May 21, 1856, John Brown, a drifter and militant abolitionist from Torrington, Connecticut, began to brood about the sack of the town. A white man, Brown nonetheless had become obsessed with the idea of taking some kind of overt action that would bring justice to black people. He had followed five of his sons to Kansas in 1855 and settled in Osawatomie, where he became the leader of antislavery guerrillas in the area.

HARPER'S FERRY INSURRECTION—BRINGING THE PRISONERS OUT OF THE ENGINE-HOUSE.—FROM A SKETCH BY OUR SPECIAL ARTIST.

ON OCTOBER 16, 1859, ABOLITIONIST JOHN BROWN AND A GROUP OF SIXTY MEN CAPTURED THE FEDERAL ARMORY AT HARPERS FERRY, VIRGINIA. HE AND HIS MEN WERE SOON CAPTURED, BUT JOHN BROWN BECAME A MARTYR FOR THE ANTISLAVERY CAUSE WHEN HE WAS HANGED FOR HIS ACTIONS.

Three days after the violence in Lawrence, Brown decided he had a divine mission to seek vengeance. So he led a nighttime raid against the proslavery settlement at Pottawatomie Creek. Five men were dragged from their beds and hacked to death. Several months later, Osawatomie was attacked by proslavery forces from Missouri. Brown and his followers successfully fought them off. After this, he became famous in the North as an abolitionist and gained the nickname "Old Brown of Osawatomie."

In 1858, a year after the Scott case, Brown had higher ambitions. First, he announced he would set up a stronghold in the Maryland and Virginia mountains for escaping slaves. He actually gained support for this idea from some Boston abolitionists and was elected commander in chief of the paper government. Then, in 1859, he established headquarters with a group of blacks and whites in a farmhouse across the Potomac from Harpers Ferry, Virginia, the site of a federal armory. On the night of October 16, Brown led a group of some sixty men in a raid on the armory. He believed this action would cause escaped slaves to join his rebellion.

Brown and his men did capture the arsenal and held out for a night and day against the local militia. He was finally overcome when a small force of U.S. Marines arrived, led by the future Civil War general Robert E. Lee. Brown was injured, and ten of his men, including two of his sons, were killed.

John Brown was tried and convicted in Charlestown, Virginia. His actions never brought on a rebellion among escaped slaves, but surprisingly, this abolitionist, who was regarded by many as a militant madman, spoke eloquently in his own defense. In his last speech at his trial on

November 2, 1859, Brown said,

> Now, if it is deemed necessary that I should forfeit my life for the furtherance of the ends of justice, and mingle my blood further with the blood of my children and with the blood of millions in this slave country whose rights are disregarded by wicked, cruel, and unjust enactments, I submit; so let it be done!

With his hanging on December 2, Brown became a martyr for the antislavery cause and actually helped to hasten the war.

## THE National Election

In the meantime, a series of debates had been swirling about the slavery issue between Illinois Senator Stephen A. Douglas and an unknown lawyer from Springfield, Illinois, named Abraham Lincoln. (Douglas had introduced the Kansas-Nebraska Act in 1854.) Everyone knew Douglas, a fluent, impressive orator who was running for reelection to the Senate. People did not know Lincoln, but they began to like his humor and honesty and the down-home way he spoke. He became known during the Lincoln-Douglas debates, a series of seven meetings in the course of the senatorial campaign that largely concerned the extension of slavery into the territories.

Douglas was a passionate speaker, but Lincoln more than held his own. In truth, the two men were not so very far apart on all aspects of the relationship between the black and white races. Lincoln was against slavery, but he was as horrified as Douglas at the thought of blacks and whites intermarrying. He did not plan to

ABRAHAM LINCOLN PRESIDED OVER THE BLOODIEST TIME IN UNITED STATES HISTORY. WHEN HE RAN FOR SENATOR AGAINST STEPHEN DOUGLAS, HE ARGUED THAT "A HOUSE DIVIDED AGAINST ITSELF CANNOT STAND."

attack slavery directly but to contain it. However, more than anything Lincoln defended his country, and he was convinced that, if continued, slavery would tear it apart.

In his nomination speech at the Republican State Convention, Lincoln said, "A house divided against itself cannot stand. I believe this government cannot endure permanently half slave and half free." In continuing, he brought up the three issues that had kept Dred Scott a slave:

> First, that no negro slave . . . can ever be a citizen of any State. . . . This point is made in order to deprive the negro, in every possible event, of the benefit of that provision of the United States Constitution, which declares that "The citizens of each State, shall be entitled to all privileges and immunities of citizens in several States."

> Secondly, that . . . neither Congress nor a Territorial Legislature can exclude slavery from any United States territory. This point is made in order that individual men may fill up the territories with slaves. . . .

> Thirdly, that whether the holding a negro in actual slavery in a free State, makes him free. . . . This point is made . . . to sustain the logical conclusion that what Dred Scott's master might lawfully do with Dred Scott, in the free State of Illinois, every other master may lawfully do with any other one, or one thousand slaves, in Illinois, or in any other free State.

THIS CARTOON DEPICTS CANDIDATE ABRAHAM LINCOLN LEAPING OVER RIVAL
STEPHEN DOUGLAS IN THEIR 1856 SENATORIAL RACE DEBATES. NEVERTHELESS,
DOUGLAS WON THE ELECTION.

At the second debate, held in Freeport, Illinois, on August 27, 1858, Lincoln cleverly used the *Dred Scott* decision to make Douglas take a stand on slavery. Among many questions, Lincoln asked Douglas if people in a U.S. territory could exclude slavery before the state constitution for that territory was formed. Douglas did not want to answer. The Supreme Court, in deciding the *Dred Scott* case, had ruled that Congress had no power to prohibit slavery in the territories. The answer should have been no, but Douglas did not want to say that and anger his northern supporters, whom he needed. Yet he certainly did not want to alienate the South. Instead, he answered by saying that slavery could not exist unless supported by the local police regulations and that a territory can exclude slavery by unfriendly laws. Disgusted with the reply, southerners began to call his answer the Freeport Doctrine.

In the end, despite the Freeport Doctrine, the impassioned veteran won out over the eloquent newcomer, and Douglas returned to the Senate. However, that was the last election Abe Lincoln would ever lose. He was nominated to run for the presidency on the third ballot of the Republican National Convention in May 1860. Hannibal Hamlin of Maine, a former Democrat, was his running mate. However, the Democrats were split. Douglas was nominated by the regular (northern) Democrats, while the southerners supported John C. Breckinridge as the candidate for the so-called National Democrats. John Bell of Tennessee ran as the candidate for the Constitutional Union Party.

The Republicans were firmly behind Lincoln, but the Democrats were in disarray. Lincoln did not run an active campaign. He made no stump speeches; he had said all he had to say on the issue of slavery. In one of the country's most important national elections, Lincoln won with 40 percent of the popular vote because the country was so split by sectional issues. He took 180 electoral votes over 72 for Breckinridge, 39 for Bell, and 12 for Douglas. No one in the Deep South voted for Lincoln.

Abraham Lincoln was elected the sixteenth president of the United States on November 6, 1860. A little more than a month later, on December 20, South Carolina, fearful that Lincoln would destroy the South, seceded from the Union. Lincoln was inaugurated on March 4, 1861. By that time, six more states, Alabama, Florida, Georgia, Louisiana, Mississippi, and Texas, had joined South Carolina to form the Confederate States of America. The new president declared in his inaugural speech that secession was unlawful and appealed to the South to return. Despite Lincoln's appeal, the South established a provisional government at Montgomery, Alabama, and installed Jefferson Davis as the new president. The new government operated under a structure similar to that of the United States. The Confederacy soon had its own stamps and flag, called the Stars and Bars. Then, on April 12 Confederate forces fired on the federal military post of Fort Sumter in the harbor of Charleston, South Carolina. At that time, South Carolina was joined by four other states of the upper South: Arkansas, North Carolina, Tennessee, and Virginia. The long-dreaded, inevitable civil war, hastened by a decision over a slave named Dred Scott, had begun.

## LINCOLN AND TANEY

The Civil War would rage for four long, bloody years. An estimated 600,000 Americans died in the fight before it ended with a Union victory at Appomattox Court House, Virginia, on April 7, 1865. During the war and until his death in December 1864, Taney clashed many times with the president of the United States. In failing health and bitter over the harsh reaction to his decision in the *Dred Scott* case, Taney fought Lincoln on almost every use he made of the power of the federal government.

One such clash between the two was over an incident involving John Merryman, a Confederate sympathizer in Maryland, which was one of four border states. Along with Delaware, Kentucky, and Missouri, Maryland remained in the Union but was a pro-South slave state. Merryman was arrested for participating in the destruction of railroad bridges. In May 1861, Merryman was held without charge at Fort McHenry because Lincoln had suspended habeas corpus (literally, "you shall have the body"), which requires that an accused person be brought before a court or judge. Lincoln suspended the writ, claiming he had the authority to do so in wartime to stop antiwar activities by sympathizers and demonstrators. Taney disagreed. When the chief justice issued a writ ordering General George Cadwalader at Fort McHenry to turn Merryman over to the federal court, the general refused, saying that the president had the authority to suspend the writ in wartime.

An angry chief justice then wrote an opinion, *Ex parte Merryman*, in which he declared that Congress—not the president—held such power. Lincoln's attorney general disagreed. Lincoln stood his ground, although some time later he did allow Merryman to be released to a federal court for trial. Merryman was indicted for treason but was released on bond and never went to court.

The Merryman incident was only one of several instances where Taney was at odds with Lincoln. On April 19, 1861, Lincoln ordered a blockade of the southern coast to seize ships that were trading with the South. To be legal, a blockade had to be issued in time of war—and only Congress had the authority to declare war. As Congress was not in session at the time, it did not order the blockade until July 13. However, the administration argued that the power given to Congress in the Constitution concerned only "foreign" war and that the president had been correct in taking immediate steps to act on the southern rebellion. It was a narrow squeak, but the Supreme Court agreed. Taney dissented. He also thought Lincoln's Conscription Act to draft men for the army was illegal, and he disagreed with the president's Emancipation Proclamation, which freed the slaves on January 1, 1863. On that point, many historians agree with Taney. As president, Lincoln had no authority to issue such a declaration. In his role as commander in chief of the military, he could issue an order only if it pertained to territory within his own lines. The proclamation applied only to territory outside his lines: "the States and parts of States wherein the people thereof, respectively, are this day in rebellion against the United States. . . ."

Legal or not, the Emancipation Proclamation turned the war from one aimed primarily at preserving the Union into a crusade for human freedom. On a practical level, it gave a go-ahead signal to recruit black soldiers. Nearly 180,000 blacks wore the Union blue during the rest of the war.

The war between Lincoln and Taney ended before the end of the Civil War. Taney died in Washington, D.C., on October 12, 1864, at the age of eighty-seven. His long career was forever dogged by the *Dred Scott* case. A long funeral procession, which included Lincoln and members of

Congress, walked to the train depot and—with the exception of the president and a few cabinet members—left for Frederick, Maryland. At his request, Taney was buried beside his mother in the Catholic cemetery.

Abraham Lincoln would be reelected to a second term in 1864. He lived long enough to see the end of the terrible conflict but not long enough to help heal the wounds. Lincoln was shot by John Wilkes Booth at Ford's Theatre in Washington, D.C., on April 14, 1865, and died the following day.

## WHEN SLAVERY DIED

The Civil War was fought mainly over the issue of slavery. At its end, the approximately four million former slaves in the United States were free. What did "free" mean? What could they do with their freedom?

Like Dred Scott, most slaves were illiterate. Very few had real skills beyond those needed to work in the plantation fields. They might rejoice at the idea of being free, but they had very few resources to sustain them once they left the plantations. Thus, many freed slaves did not leave but instead continued to work for the people who had formerly been their owners.

Most slaves had never earned money, bought goods in a store, or purchased a railroad ticket. Their new freedom left them without jobs or money and nowhere to go. During the so-called period of Reconstruction (1865–1877) following the war, the federal government tried to deal with the political, social, and economic problems that arose. Constitutional amendments that gave legal force to the new freedom of the former slaves were passed, and organizations—such as the Freedmen's Bureau, which the South bitterly resented—were set up to

# The New-York Times.

VOL. XIV.....NO. 4167.     NEW-YORK, WEDNESDAY, FEBRUARY 1, 1865.     PRICE FOUR CENTS.

THE THIRD COLUMN FROM THE LEFT OF THE FEBRUARY 1, 1865, EDITION OF *THE NEW YORK TIMES* MARKS THE ABOLITION OF SLAVERY.

help feed, protect, and educate the newly emancipated slaves. The resentment felt by the South helped hasten the formation of such secret antiblack societies as the Ku Klux Klan and the Knights of the White Camelia. The Ku Klux Klan was formed in 1866 by Confederate veterans in Tennessee. It quickly became a vehicle for resistance to Reconstruction in the South. Another society that was similar in outlook and structure, the Knights of the White Camelia, was organized in Louisiana in 1867. By 1877 Southern opponents of Reconstruction had once again gained control of their state governments. The Democratic Party was back in power nationally, and the last of the federal troops had been withdrawn.

Although the Civil War settled the question of slavery in the United States, the Reconstruction experience was so bitter that it increased sectional animosity and intensified the issue of race. The repercussions of that period are still felt in the United States. Historians say the fundamental failing of Reconstruction was that it did not deal with a distribution of land, which would have given former slaves an economic base to go with their newly won political rights.

## Free at Last

The long fight for freedom by Dred Scott and many other American blacks was not satisfed—at least in a legal sense—until the Thirteenth and Fourteenth Amendments to the U.S. Constitution were ratified on December 6, 1865, and July 9, 1868, respectively. The Thirteenth Amendment states, "Neither slavery nor involuntary servitude, except as a punishment for crime whereof the party shall have been duly convicted, shall exist within the United States, or any place subject to their jurisdiction." According to the Fourteenth Amendment,

> All persons born or naturalized in the United States, and subject to the jurisdiction thereof, are citizens of the United States and of the State wherein they reside. No State shall make or enforce any law which shall abridge the privileges or immunities of citizens of the United States; nor shall any State deprive any person of life, liberty, or property, without due process of law; nor deny to any person within its jurisdiction the equal protection of the laws.

Both of these amendments effectively overruled the decision in *Scott* v. *Sandford*.

*Due process*, as noted in the Fourteenth Amendment, refers to the rules and principles established in a legal system to enforce and protect private rights. The term's meaning has changed over years of interpretation, mostly controversial, by the Supreme Court. In modern terms, a law meets the due process standard if it may be seen as promoting the public welfare and if the means through which it operates have a reasonable relationship to the public interest.

The case of *Scott* v. *Sandford* lives on through its place in the legal history of the United States. It is one of several Supreme Court decisions that are landmark cases. First among them is *Marbury* v. *Madison* (1803), which established the Supreme Court as arbiter of the U.S. Constitution. Another is *Plessy* v. *Ferguson* (1896), in which the Supreme Court accepted racial segregation by endorsing the idea of "separate but equal." The one dissenting justice, John Marshall Harlan, said that this decision would "defeat the beneficent purposes" of the Thirteenth and Fourteenth amendments. It took almost sixty years before racial segregation was overturned by *Brown* v. *Board of Education*, which desegregated American schools in 1954.

Another landmark case is *Roe* v. *Wade* in 1973, which legalized abortion and is still highly controversial. The bearing of *Dred Scott* on *Roe* is that the latter case continued the tradition set by the Court in 1867 of substantive due process based on its power of judicial review. In *Dred Scott*, the right of owners (slaveholders) to their property (slaves) under the Fifth Amendment was upheld against a federal law; in *Roe*, women's "right to privacy" was upheld under the Fourteenth Amendment's concept of personal liberty against state laws prohibiting abortion.

Through the years, these and other decisions by the Court have brought profound changes to the history of the nation and the lives of American citizens. Part of the legacy of *Scott* v. *Sandford* is that it is generally regarded as the worst decision ever handed down by the Supreme Court and the worst failure of the U.S. judicial system.

# TIMELINE

**1800**    On or around this date, Dred Scott is born a slave in Virginia to family of Peter Blow

**1820**    Missouri Compromise passed; Missouri admitted to the Union as a slave state, Maine as a free state

**1830**    Blow family moves to St. Louis, Missouri, taking Scott with them

**1831**    Elizabeth Blow dies

**1832**    Peter Blow dies; Scott bought by Dr. John Emerson, an army surgeon

**1833 or 1834**    Emerson takes Scott to military post at Fort Armstrong, Illinois, free territory

**1836**    Wisconsin Territory established April 20, including present-day Minnesota; Emerson takes Scott to new assignment, Fort Snelling (present-day Minnesota); Scott marries slave Harriet Robinson

**1837**    Emerson transferred to Fort Jesup, Louisiana; leaves Scott and wife behind

**1838** Emerson marries Irene Sanford, sends for Scott and wife; all four return to Fort Snelling in October; Scotts' first child, Eliza, born on Mississippi riverboat; Emerson reassigned to Florida; leaves wife and Scotts in St. Louis

**1842** Emerson discharged from the army, moves to Iowa territory; Scotts remain in St. Louis

**1843** Emerson dies; his wife becomes the Scotts' new owner

**1846** Scotts' second daughter, Lizzie, born; Dred and Harriet Scott file for freedom on grounds he had lived in free territory and was, therefore, free

**1847** Trial denies freedom on a technicality

**1848** Scott granted new trial in St. Louis circuit court

**1850** In retrial, Scott is declared free

**1852** Irene Emerson appeals decision; Missouri Supreme Court reverses decision, declares Scott still a slave

**1853** New suit in Missouri federal court names John F. A. Sanford as defendant

**1854** Kansas-Nebraska Act opens new territory to slavery; Scott loses again in court; remains a slave

**1856–1857** U.S. Supreme Court declares Dred Scott has always been a slave, therefore, is not a U.S. citizen, and will remain a slave; Court also declares Missouri Compromise unconstitutional

1857    John Sanford dies; Emerson returns Scotts to
        Blow family, who give them their freedom

1858    Dred Scott dies, is buried in St. Louis

1865    Thirteenth Amendment abolishes slavery

1868    Fourteenth Amendment gives citizenship to all
        those born in the United States regardless of race

1869    Fifteenth Amendment prohibits voting
        discrimination on basis of race

# NOTES

## Chapter 1

p. 7, par.1, Walker Lewis. *Without Fear or Favor: A Biography of Chief Justice Roger Brooke Taney*. Boston: Houghton-Mifflin, 1965, p. 401.

p. 7, par. 2, Kermit L. Hall, ed. *The Oxford Companion to the Supreme Court of the United States*. New York: Oxford University Press, 1992, p. 759.

p. 9, par. 1, Don E. Fehrenbacher. *The Dred Scott Case: Its Significance in American Law and Politics*. New York: Oxford University Press, 1978, p. 240.

p. 12, par. 4, Ibid., p. 245.

p. 13, par. 1, Paul Finkelman. *Dred Scott v. Sandford: A Brief History with Documents*. New York: St. Martins, 1997, p. 19.

p. 16, par. 1, Walter Ehrlich. "The Origins of the Dred Scott Case," *Journal of Negro History* 59, no. 2 (April 1974): 134.

p. 16, par. 2, "Five 'Little' People Who Changed U.S. History." *Scholastic Update* 122, no. 10 (January 26, 1999): 8+.

## Chapter 2

p. 37, par. 2, Kermit L. Hall, ed. *The Oxford Companion to the Supreme Court of the United States*. New York: Oxford University Press, 1992, p. 796.

p. 38, par. 4, Paul Finkelman. *Dred Scott v. Sandford: A Brief History with Documents*. New York: St. Martins, 1997, p. 22.

p. 39, par. 1, Don E. Fehrenbacher. *The Dred Scott Case: Its Significance in American Law and Politics*. New York: Oxford University Press, 1978, p. 265.

p. 42, par. 4, Finekelman, *Dred Scott v. Sandford*, p. 25.

p. 46, par. 3, Fehrenbacher, *The Dred Scott Case*, p. 280.

p. 46, par. 5, Ibid.

## Chapter 3

p. 66, par. 3, Kermit L. Hall, ed. *The Oxford Companion to the Supreme Court of the United States*. New York: Oxford University Press, 1992, p. 858.

p. 66, par. 5, Walker Lewis. *Without Fear or Favor: A Biography of Chief Justice Roger Brooke Taney*. Boston: Houghton Mifflin, 1965, p. 269.

p. 67, par. 3, Ibid., p. 277.

## Chapter 4

p. 77, par. 1, Don E. Fehrenbacher. *The Dred Scott Case: Its Significance in American Law and Politics*. New York: Oxford University Press, 1978, p. 313.

p. 77, par. 3, Walker Lewis. *Without Fear or Favor: A Biography of Chief Justice Roger Brooke Taney*. Boston: Houghton Mifflin, 1965, p. 396.

p. 83, par. 3, Paul Finkelman. *Dred Scott v. Sandford: A Brief History with Documents*. New York: St. Martins, 1997, p. 56.

p. 84, par. 4, Ibid., p. 35.

p. 85, par. 3, Lewis. *Without Fear or Favor*, p. 317.

p. 87, par. 2, Ibid., p. 319.

p. 89, par. 2, Walter Ehrlich. *They Have No Rights: Dred Scott's Struggle for Freedom*.Westport, CT: Greenwood, 1979, p. 182.

p. 89, par. 3, www.pbs.org, August 17, 2003.

## Chapter 5

p. 92, par. 1, http://history.furman.edu, August 20, 2003.

p. 92, par. 2, www.digitalhistory.uh.edu, August 18, 2003.

p. 92, par. 2, Vincent C. Hopkins. *Dred Scott's Case*. New York: Atheneum, 1971, p. 163.

p. 99, par. 1, Walker Lewis. *Without Fear or Favor: A Biography of Chief Justice Roger Brooke Taney*. Boston: Houghton Mifflin, 1965, p. 421.

p. 101, par. 1, www.tncrimlaw.com/civil_bible/John_brown.htm, August 20, 2003.

p. 101, par. 1, "The History Place," www.historyplace.com/lincoln/divided/htm, August 20, 2003, pp. 2–3.

p. 101, par. 2, Ibid.

p. 106, par. 1, www.hypermall.com/LibertyOnly/Lincoln/emancipate.htm, August 21, 2003, p. 1.

# furTHer InformaTIon

## Books

Altman, Linda. *Slavery and Abolition*. Berkeley Heights, NJ: Enslow, 1999.

Freedman, Suzanne. *Roger Taney: The Dred Scott Legacy*. Berkeley Heights, NJ: Enslow, 1995.

Greenberg, Ellen. *The Supreme Court Explained*. New York: Norton, 1997.

Hamilton,Virginia. *Many Thousand Gone: African Americans from Slavery to Freedom*. New York: Random House, 1993.

January, Brendan. *The Dred Scott Decision*. New York: Scholastic, 1998.

Lester, Julius. *To Be a Slave*. New York: Scholastic, 1968.

Lutz, Norma Jean. *Harriet Tubman: Leader of the Underground Railroad*. New York: Chelsea, 2001.

Patrick, John J. *The Supreme Court of the United States: A Student's Companion*. New York: Oxford University Press, 2001.

## Web Sites

Abraham Lincoln's "House Divided" Speech
www.historyplace.com/lincoln/divided.htm

Abraham Lincoln's Speeches
www.hypermall.com/LibertyOnline/Lincoln/

Digital History
www.digitalhistory.uh.edu

Dred Scott case: The Supreme Court decision
www.pbs.org/wgbh/aia/part4/4h2933.html

Washington University Libraries *Dred Scott* case materials
http:library.wustl.edu/ulib/dredscott/toc.html

# BIBLIOGraPHY

## Books

Ehrlich, Walter. *They Have No Rights: Dred Scott's Struggle for Freedom*. Westport, CT: Greenwood, 1979.

Fehrenbacher, Don E. *The Dred Scott Case: Its Significance in American Law and Politics*. New York: Oxford University Press, 1978.

Finkelman, Paul. *Dred Scott v. Sandford: A Brief History with Documents*. New York: St. Martins, 1997.

Hall, Kermit L., ed. *The Oxford Companion to the Supreme Court of the United States*. New York: Oxford University Press, 1992.

Hopkins, Vincent C. *Dred Scott's Case*. New York: Atheneum, 1971.

Kutler, Stanley I. *The Dred Scott Decision: Law or Politics?* Boston: Houghton Mifflin, 1967.

Lewis, Walter. *Without Fear or Favor: A Biography of Roger Brooke Taney*. Boston: Houghton Mifflin, 1965.

Stowe, Harriet Beecher. *Uncle Tom's Cabin*. New York: Bantam, 1982.

**Articles**

Ehrlich, Walter. "The Origins of the Dred Scott Case." *Journal of Negro History* 59, no. 2 (April 1974).

———. "Was the Dred Scott Case Valid?" *Journal of American History* 55, no. 2 (September 1968).

"Five 'Little' People Who Changed U.S. History." *Scholastic Update* 122, no. 10 (January 26, 1990).

# index

Page numbers in **boldface** are illustrations, tables, and charts

## ABOUT THe AUTHOrS

**Corinne J. Naden** is a former U.S. Navy journalist and children's book editor. The author of more than eighty nonfiction books for young readers, she lives in Tarrytown, New York. *Marbury v. Madison: The Court's Foundation*, and *Dred Scott: Person or Property?* are her first titles for Benchmark Books.

**Rose Blue**, a native of Brooklyn, New York, has published more than eighty fiction and nonfiction books for young readers. Two of them have been adapted and aired by NBC television network. *Marbury v. Madison: The Court's Foundation*, and *Dred Scott: Person or Property?* are also her first titles for Benchmark Books.